THE DISCOVERED SELF

THE SEARCH FOR SELF-ACCEPTANCE

Earl D. Wilson

INTERVARSITY PRESS
DOWNERS GROVE, ILLINOIS 60515

InterVarsity Press is the book-publishing division of Inter-Varsity Christian Fellowship, a student movement active on campus at hundreds of universities, colleges and schools of nursing. For information about local and regional activities, write IVCF, 233 Langdon St., Madison, WI 53703.

Distributed in Canada through InterVarsity Press, 860 Denison St., Unit 3, Markham, Ontario L3R 4H1, Canada.

Scripture taken from the Holy Bible: New International Version. Copyright © 1973, 1978 by the International Bible Society. Used by permission of Zondervan Bible Publishers.

Cover illustration: Roberta Polfus

ISBN 0-87784-331-7

Printed in the United States of America

Library of Congress Cataloging in Publication Data

Wilson, Earl D., 1939-
  The discovered self.

  Bibliography: p.
  1. Self-acceptance—religious aspects—Christianity.
2. Self. I. Title.
BV4509.5.W495   1985   248.4   84-28943
ISBN 0-87784-331-7

16   15   14   13   12   11   10   9   8   7   6   5   4   3   2
99   98   97   96   95   94   93   92   91   90   89   88   87   86   85

*This book is affectionately dedicated to
Maude Cooper and Herschel Gregg,
whose skillful work with me
as Sunday-school teachers during my youth
helped me to discover myself.*

Thanks so much to both of you.

1
Is Self-Worth Unchristian?

JOAN IS NINETEEN and by most people's standards is bright and attractive. But she has trouble admitting to herself that she has any value. She told me a long and bitter story about trying to share good feelings about herself with her parents when she was a child. Her parents responded, "Remember, Joan, there is nothing good in you. God is the only person that is good."

Joan submitted to her parents' view although something within her told her they were wrong. As she grew older and became more conscious of her own sin and shortcomings, the voice within grew ever more faint. Finally, at a time when she was struggling the most, she attended a meeting on campus where the speaker said, "You will never have peace of mind until you accept the fact that you are totally rotten. Nothing in you is good. You must die to yourself. You must recognize that you are a worm."

Joan met with the speaker after the meeting and tried hard to recognize her worthlessness, as he directed. She felt better for a time, but then the bottom dropped out. Somehow being "dead" only made her feel like she wanted to die. She wasn't experiencing any of the new life that was supposed to come from the death of the old person. She was falling fast, and she had no inner resources to pull herself up with. She gave up her faith for a time and decided to "live like hell." After six months of defying her former beliefs, she decided the answer might be found in psychology. Joan wanted desperately to understand her confused feelings.

When Joan and I talked for the first time, I heard nothing but anger. She hated not only herself, but almost everyone with whom she had contact. She mentioned going to her minister when she felt the lowest. She saw him as her last hope. His solution to her dilemma might have sparked suicide, but instead it sparked hatred. The minister said, "Well, Joan, you have to go back to basics. When are you going to stop trying to control your own life? Here, read this book and we'll talk about it next time."

Joan was partway through the book before she realized it was one more call to selflessness. Hearing the message again only confused her more. By the time she got through trying to discuss the book with her pastor, she was livid. "How can that pompous ass sit there and tell me I have to be a worm?" she cried. "I know more about self-hatred than he will ever know. I used to think God was concerned about people, and I find he only loves worms. In fact, I'm not sure he loves them—maybe he only wants to torture them."

It took several weeks before Joan could work through her anger. Every time she was nearly calmed down, she would re-member something else that had been said or done to her and the trouble would start again.

As Joan's self-understanding increased through the counsel-ing process, she needed to sort out her thoughts and feelings about God. She maintained her basic belief in God, but her perceptions of who God is were very distorted. At first she couldn't read Scripture because she was still too angry. However, I challenged her to take a fresh look at God's love and at what he wanted for her. This was difficult for Joan. She could not believe that "God's best" for her was any more than her distorted view of what it means to die to self. But as we studied passages such as John 21, I encouraged her to look at the firm but loving way Jesus dealt with people. Peter, for example, was so self-centered he denied Jesus three times, and yet Jesus said, "Feed my sheep. . . . Follow me." Joan's view of God as the worm torturer began to fade. A new picture was coming into view.

As Joan began to allow herself to see God's love, she was able to pray again. She cried as she asked God for forgiveness, and she cried as she told him she wanted to forgive those who had wronged her. Behind the tears were the beginnings of a person made new. Joan's discovery of self was beginning.

Joan and I spent hours talking about strengths and weaknesses, spiritual gifts and lack of faith. She was looking for self-worth, but as she said, "Sometimes I think it's the pot of gold at the end of the rainbow."

Discovering Self-Worth

In working with Joan and others I have learned several important steps toward making self-worth a reality.

Acknowledging feelings. Discovering self-worth usually begins by acknowledging feelings. Low self-esteem is usually accompanied by fear and anger which must be faced openly and expressed openly to God. It also helps to talk to someone who will listen. Anger does not need to be acted on, but it does need to be acknowledged. You need to become aware of the ways in which fear, anger and other emotions affect your view of self.

Taking a new look at God. Once anger and other emotions are brought into the open, it is imperative to take a new look at who God is. When we are disappointed by people, interestingly

9

enough, we often make God the object of anger, fear and rejection. The God we perceive is not the God of Scripture but a lesser being created out of our frustration. When our God is small, we also will feel small and insignificant. When I feel low, I am helped by David's words in Psalm 121:1-2:

I lift up my eyes to the hills—
where does my help come from?
My help comes from the LORD,
The Maker of heaven and earth.

Tearfully Joan said, "God, you are OK. I'm just denying you because I'm afraid."

Taking a new look at self. Joan had not only reduced God, but also herself. She had to learn to be honest with herself about herself. If you want to discover self-worth, you must learn to tell it like it is. What are your strengths and weaknesses? Who is this person God has made? Self-worth does not come from viewing only our strengths. It comes from seeing that we have strengths even when we feel weak. Joan was depressed and couldn't get herself together. She didn't need to become less. She needed to see that God had made her a worthwhile person and had given her valuable gifts. What she needed now was guidance to help her decide how to use the worth she had.

Avoiding the comparison trap. From the beginning of time men and women have wanted to know all and do all. Adam and Eve ate of the forbidden tree in order to acquire all knowledge, to become equal with God. Later Cain killed Abel, jealous because God preferred his brother's sacrifice. The issue in both instances is comparison. We are all tempted to evaluate our self-worth by comparing ourselves with someone else, but this is a great trap. Comparisons are a curse for someone who is trying to understand and accept himself or herself. Paul the apostle offers a blunt warning. "We do not dare to classify or compare ourselves with some who commend themselves. When they measure themselves by themselves and compare themselves with themselves, they are not wise" (2 Cor 10:12).

The Christian life is a team sport. Each member of the team has a role to fill, and Christ our captain understands how important each player is. He also wants the players to recognize how important they are so they can enjoy playing the game. The Christian team has suffered from low morale for too long. Imagine Christ introducing his team by saying, "This is Joan. She has value to us because she is a worm. And besides that, she is not as good a player as Jill. This is Pete. I don't know why we haven't cut him from the team because he is not as good as Mark." In truth Christ has said through Paul:

Just as each of us has one body with many members, and these members do not all have the same function, so in Christ we who are many form one body, and each member belongs to all the others. We have different gifts, according to the grace given us. If a man's gift is prophesying, let him use it in proportion to his faith. If it is serving, let him serve; if it is teaching, let him teach; if it is encouraging, let him encourage; if it is contributing to the needs of others, let him give generously; if it is leadership, let him govern diligently; if it is showing mercy, let him do it cheerfully. (Rom 12:4-8)

I hope that one additional Scripture will clearly alert you to the comparison trap. In Galatians 6 the apostle Paul gives instruction on how to restore a brother who is caught in a sin. In this passage we are told that we are to examine ourselves because each person must learn to be responsible for himself or herself. "For each one should carry his own load" (v. 5). The remarkable part comes in verse 4. Paul writes, "Each one should test his own actions. Then he can take pride in himself, without comparing himself to somebody else."

The passage clearly says that as we examine ourselves, God intends us to boast about ourselves. We can be really proud of what he is doing in us and what he is enabling us to do. (Isn't that what team captains or coaches are for?) Once again, though, the warning is sounded. We are to rejoice in ourselves alone—not in comparison to others. People don't usually have trouble with pride when they look at themselves by themselves. It is only when they make comparisons that they are overcome with pride. Comparisons can be destructive in another way also: when we compare, we tend to want to bring the other person down to our size. Scripture clearly tells us to give each person his or her proper place. "Now we ask you, brothers, to respect those who work hard among you, who are over you in the Lord and who admonish you. Hold them in the highest regard in love because of their work. Live in peace with each other" (1 Thess 5:12-13). People who feel good about themselves can more easily praise the good in others. But be sure that you watch out for the comparison trap. It will rob you of the joy of seeing your own worth, and it will also rob you of the excitement of lifting someone else higher.

If you challenge the you-must-be-a-worm approach as I have done, you still need to understand what Scripture means when it says we must die to self. Dying to self needs to be understood in light of the biblical teaching about servanthood, self-worth and selfishness. We will look at a key passage in each of these three areas.

On Being a Servant

Entering the reception area of my office, I could hear Gail, my office manager, singing as she arranged supplies in the storage room. The tune caught my attention, and I paused to listen. The words were from the Gospels: "If you want to be great in God's kingdom, you have to be the servant of all." I went to my office, dragged out my concordance, and looked at the entries under *servant*. I found these words in Mark 9:35: "Sitting down, Jesus called the Twelve and said, 'If anyone wants to be first, he must be the very last, and the servant of all.' "

I smiled as I thought of those words and Gail's life. She truly has a servant's heart, and yet she does not suffer from low self-esteem. She knows who she is and doesn't feel less when she serves others. Serving others is a choice she makes, and it seems to increase her self-esteem rather than tear it down.

Jesus himself made that choice. Notice these words:

Your attitude should be the same as that of Christ Jesus: Who, being in very nature God, did not consider equality with God something to be grasped, but made himself nothing, taking the very nature of a servant, being made in human likeness. And being found in appearance as a man, he humbled himself and became obedient to death—even death on a cross! Therefore God exalted him to the highest place and gave him the name that is above every name, that at the name of Jesus every knee should bow, in heaven and on earth and under the earth, and every tongue confess that Jesus Christ is Lord, to the glory of God the Father. (Phil 2:5-11)

Jesus deliberately chose the servant's role in order to care for us. By his death he made our return to God possible, and by his unselfish life he showed us how to live. Did he have to give up his self-esteem to do that? I don't think so. Even at age twelve he said, "Why were you searching for me? Didn't you know I had to be in my Father's house?" (Lk 2:49). This sounds to me like a positive affirmation of worth. Jesus knew who he was, even though he accepted the lowly servant role.

Bruce Narramore points out:

The Greek word that is transliterated "ego" simply means "I." Used over three hundred times in the New Testament, it means nothing more or less than "I." It is used by Christ, John the Baptist, Luke, John and Paul, and has absolutely no negative connotation.

Jesus, for example, speaks of Himself in this way. During His Sermon on the Mount, He said, "But I [Greek, "ego"] tell you, Love your enemies and pray for those who persecute you" (Matt. 5:44). Jesus had an ego too! Jesus not only had an ego; He was an ego.[1]

Philippians 2:1-4 shows us how trying to be like Christ should affect our behavior:

If you have any encouragement from being united with

Christ, if any comfort from his love, if any fellowship with the Spirit, if any tenderness and compassion, then make my joy complete by being like-minded, having the same love, being one in spirit and purpose. Do nothing out of selfish ambition or vain conceit, but in humility consider others better than yourselves. Each of you should look not only to your own interests, but also to the interests of others. (Phil 2:1-4)

The biblical imperative to be a servant of God and others is clear. We, like Christ, are to serve. But worms are not usually good servants because they do not have the strength of character to look out for the interests of others when they are struggling for psychological survival themselves. Scripture does not teach that you have to be worthless before you can be a servant. This idea is a human invention. It's not God's. There is a strong inference in Philippians that we are able to serve as Christ did because of our sense of self and purpose rather than out of a sense of weakness. Paul wrote, "Though I am free and belong to no man, I make myself a slave to everyone, to win as many as possible" (1 Cor 9:19).

The Source of Self-Worth

I have found that many Christians have trouble saying, "I am worthy; I am capable." We are taught that it is wrong to accept credit for the things we can do. But this presents a problem. To deny that you are worthy is to label the Creator's work unacceptable. When God finished his creation, including man, he was satisfied: "God saw all that he had made, and it was very good" (Gen 1:31). It is unfortunate that we do not maintain that same satisfaction with ourselves. We are made in God's image and likeness, and we have been given dominion over the rest of creation. God would not give you and me such responsibility without giving us the capacity to carry it out. Recently I read the autobiography of Herbert J. Taylor, used by God to help establish several nondenominational ministries to youth in the United States. Taylor was a humble man, and yet he realized that God had made him capable of handling each day's task. His humility did not come at the expense of his self-worth.

Bob, a client of mine, listened to my sermonette about self-worth. When I was finished he said, "That's fine, but you seem to have left out one point. Man sinned." Bob was so right. Man not only sinned but individual men and women keep on sinning. How can we be worthy when we are marred by a terrible tendency to be less than who God intended us to be?

I tried to help Bob to realize that that is what redemption is all about. Christ died to buy us back from slavery to sin so that we can resume being the worthy people God created us to be. Notice 2 Corinthians 5:17-18: "Therefore, if anyone is in Christ, he is a new creation; the old has gone, the new has come! All this is from God, who reconciled us to himself through Christ and gave us the ministry of reconciliation." A relationship with Jesus Christ restores us to the place where we can once again use the potential God has placed within us. When we are in Christ, we don't have to wait for a miracle to realize we are worthy. We are free to live out the goodness God placed within us at both Creation and re-creation.

"Bob," I said, "you don't have to prove to God that you are adequate. You need to allow God to prove to you that you are adequate."

"That's hard!" Bob replied. "It is easier to think of myself as a nerd. Then I don't have to try to accomplish anything."

Scripture speaks directly about self-worth and adequacy: "Such confidence as this is ours through Christ before God. Not that we are competent to claim anything for ourselves, but our competence comes from God. He has made us competent as ministers of a new covenant" (2 Cor 3:4-6). The issue in this passage is not competence; that is taken for granted. The issue is, who is the source of our competence? The last part of verse 5 nails it down: "Our competence comes from God." How can you read these verses and say you are unworthy, inadequate, incompetent? At times you may feel woefully inadequate; however, by trusting God and moving forward even during periods of self-doubt, you will find that he has given you more competence than you realize. I believe that one reason the positive-thinking movement has made an impact is that it challenges people to step out. When people step out into the difficult areas of life, they discover that God has made them out of good material. At first Bob was afraid to try to accomplish anything, but as he took the risk of believing he could be more than he was, he grew.

In 2 Corinthians 9:8 Paul writes about God's provision for our needs: "God is able to make all grace abound to you, so that in all things at all times, having all that you need, you will abound in every good work." God doesn't make us adequate simply to serve our own purposes or satisfy our own egos. He gives us adequacy so that we may serve him and our fellow men and women. It is interesting that the word *autarkeia*, used in the phrase "having all that you need," can be translated self-satisfaction or contentedness or competency. Recognizing that God has given you value and realizing that you are adequate should result in a higher quality of life—a contented life. As Bob came to realize both intellectually and emotionally that he was adequate, he began to enjoy life more. In a moment of productive introspection he said, "I've spent too much of my life trying to prove I was OK rather than just being OK."

Notice 1 Timothy 6:6, "Godliness with contentment is great gain." The word translated "contentment" is the same word *autarkeia*. The verse does not say godliness is great gain. That is true, but the greatest gain comes when godliness is combined with the awareness of self-worth.

I have known too many people who are godly and miserable. I believe their misery often results from their refusal to accept their self-worth. Just as godliness requires you and me to make right choices, so does contentment. The first right choice that leads to contentment is to realize that God has made us adequate.

The Problem of Selfishness

I have discovered an interesting thing about selfish people. They do not feel loved. In fact, the more selfish they are, the less love they feel; and the less loved they feel, the more selfish they become. It is a vicious circle.

Webster defines selfish as "concerned excessively or exclusively with oneself: seeking or concentrating on one's own advantage, pleasure, or well-being without regard for others."[2]

This definition helps us understand why selfishness is condemned in Scripture while servanthood and self-worth are both encouraged. We are not to be concerned exclusively or excessively with ourselves; neither are we to concentrate on our own welfare without regard for others.

Galatians 6:2 states, "Carry each other's burdens, and in this way you will fulfill the law of Christ." Clearly we must go far beyond concern for self.

In the Sermon on the Mount Jesus plainly said that we are not to be concerned with matters such as food and clothes but are to entrust those important aspects of self-preservation to God. "Do not worry, saying, 'What shall we eat?' or 'What shall we drink?' or 'What shall we wear?' For the pagans run after all these things, and your heavenly Father knows that you need them. But seek first his kingdom and his righteousness, and all these things will be given to you as well" (Mt 6:31-33). Hoarding food or clothes is undoubtedly selfish. It is a means of self-preservation which will backfire. In Matthew 10:39 Jesus states the paradox: "Whoever finds his life will lose it, and whoever loses his life for my sake will find it." Selfishness (concentrating on finding your life) results in losing it, while servanthood (losing your life for the sake of Christ) results in finding it. It has been said that you can't outgive God. I wonder if it is also true that you can't be more selfish than Satan. The more you try to serve yourself, the less satisfying life becomes.

The Old Testament gives a beautiful example of this principle. Every morning while the children of Israel were in the wilderness, God provided fresh food for them to eat. "Then Moses said to them, 'No one is to keep any of it until morning.' However, some of them paid no attention to Moses; they kept part of it until morning, but it was full of maggots and began to smell. So Moses was angry with them" (Ex 16:19-20).

The selfish person is like one who hoards manna. He or she is trying to get the advantage, but ends up with maggots. Self-worth can be a guard against selfishness. The more you realize that God has made you adequate, the more you can trust him to meet your needs as you serve him and others. Selfish people not only do not feel loved, they also do not feel worthy.

A delicate balance must be maintained. It is not selfish to have needs or to ask to have those needs fulfilled. It is only selfish to ask or expect those needs to be met when you are unwilling to be a servant to others. Paul Hauck has shown how this balance works in a family situation. He writes:

You lay back on the sofa propped up on a pillow tossing bonbons into your mouth, and give orders to your family to be quiet while they put on your favorite record, make your coffee, and open the window a bit so you can catch the cool breeze. That is being selfish, because you are expecting others to put themselves out exclusively for you with no expectation of your doing something for them. In other words, the selfish person wants something for nothing.

The self-interested person, however, may also want to rest on the sofa, eat bonbons, and want the same services but not actually be a selfish person, for there is every intention of doing something in return for those favors.

For example, what's selfish about wanting your wife to bring you a cup of coffee if you just did the dishes for her? And what's selfish about her asking you to do the dishes if she cooks the meal? And what's selfish about your asking her to open the window and to put on your favorite record if you have just come back from picking up the dry cleaning?

These are not selfish acts, they're acts of reciprocity, acts of

payment for services rendered or expected. They say that you
are important and so is your partner.[3]

True identity is not found by becoming a worm, but rather by
becoming a self-respecting servant who realizes that God has
enabled him or her, and who therefore doesn't have to rely on
selfish behavior in order to survive. When a person reaches this
point, self-worth becomes a wonderful reality. How long has it
been since you have been able to say "I like being me"?

Listen carefully and you will hear God say, "I like who you are,
and I like who you are becoming."

2
What Is an Identity Crisis?

AS A COUNSELOR I often ask people if an act or decision they are considering is consistent with who they want to be. More often than not they answer, "I'm so confused, I don't even know who I am. How do you expect me to know who I want to be?"

Knowing ourselves is one of life's most fundamental tasks, yet it seems to have everyone upset. People may not understand the psychological concept of identity very well, but they desperately want to know themselves. Erik Erikson observes, however, that an identity crisis may "turn out to be something [not] quite as fatal as it sounds."[1]

When I first began working with college students in the early sixties, I had difficulty helping them answer the question, "Who am I?" At that time, things were pretty simple in my life. I could say without hesitation, I'm Sandy Wilson's husband. I'm Claude and Emma Wilson's son. I'm a pastor. I am a psychology graduate student. I am a handball player. I am a good teacher. Later I added a new dimension: I am Marcie Wilson's father. I was even bold enough to say, I am one of God's children. Identity was for me a number of roles, and I was comfortable with them.

As I began working as a psychologist in a college setting, I became increasingly aware of the many students who did struggle with the "Who am I?" question. The more I listened, the more empathetic I became. I began to realize that for some of these students, finding their identity was a life-and-death struggle. One day as I interviewed Jane, the issue began to take on a new perspective for me.

Jane knew who she was in terms of roles. She was a daughter. She was a student. She was Jim's girlfriend. But when Jane began to talk about her behavior, her identity fell apart. A lot of things about herself she just didn't like. Her ship was flying two flags: a flag that Jane accepted and a pirate flag that she did not like at all. Jane's problem was not that she didn't know who she was, but that she could not accept the fact that she was flying two flags. She could not tolerate the ambivalence of both admiring herself and hating herself.

My experience in getting to know Jane helped me realize identity is closely tied to self-acceptance. In fact, we seem to be faced with a dilemma: we can't accept ourselves until we know who we are, and we can't know who we are until we accept ourselves. In this book I will try to point to a way out of this predicament. In so doing, I will provide additional perspective on both identity and self-acceptance.

Redefining the Crisis

For Jane the identity crisis could not be solved by asking, "Who am I?" A new question was needed. We tried several in our attempts to get to the root of her problem: Who do I want to be? Who do others think I am? Do I dare decide who I want to be? How can I be all the things I feel? How can I accept myself as I am? What is the basis for identity anyway? Jane struggled with these issues and still remained in turmoil. She was intellectually confused and emotionally drained.

To bring some order to the chaos I said, "Jane, you want an answer to the question, 'Who am I?'—right?" She nodded and I said, "OK, I'll give you an answer. You are all the things you think and feel, whether it makes any sense to you or not. You have to begin to own all the parts to your complex person. You are good and bad, intelligent but at times not too smart, beautiful and yet physically imperfect."

Jane sat stunned for several minutes, and then the tears began to flow quietly down her pale cheeks. When she spoke her words were simple, "I thought it would be easier than that."

Why couldn't it be something mysterious or magic? It is such a simple question—I just want to know who I am! But we cannot answer the identity question for ourselves because we spend so much time and energy trying to hide aspects of ourselves that we find unacceptable. We cannot meet our own expectations, and we are afraid of the expectations others have for us. Eugene Kennedy writes:

> We cannot be free when we are bound by the expectations of other people, when being ourselves might meet with disapproval and social failure. We make ourselves miserable when we live as though we were trying to avoid being blackballed at our favorite club. There is not much room left for ourselves—or for even finding out who we are—when impressing others becomes our basic style in life.[2]

Hiding our true self from others and from ourselves intensifies the identity crisis. Neither identity nor self-acceptance can be based upon a standard of perfection. You and I are not perfect! We are human. In fact, we are both human and sinful. What does that have to do with finding identity?

Earlier I said that identity and self-acceptance present problems which we cannot solve alone. It is obvious that a solid identity coupled with firm self-acceptance must have some basis beyond the turmoil we see inside ourselves. Where do we turn to find the needed affirmation of self when we cannot find it within?

A New Basis for Identity

When I married my wife, Sandy, she was as negative and insecure about herself as I was positive about myself. She wasn't sure who she was or who she wanted to be. The only thing she was really confident about was our relationship. In the years that have followed, she has grown both to know who she is and to feel good about herself in most areas. What has made the difference? I, on the other hand, have had to face some realities about myself to the point of not being so cocksure as I once was. What has made the difference there?

Sandy traces her development to her realization that she was loved and accepted by God. Her love relationship with God and to a lesser degree with me helped her see just how acceptable she really is. This allowed her to own both her strengths and her weaknesses. In my case, God had been a part of my life from early childhood, and I often took him for granted. I had to recognize my weaknesses before I could accept his love and more realistically accept all of me. Sandy and I were both growing. She had to be pushed up in order to grow while I had to be moved down a peg or two before I could grow.

It is my basic premise that there is only one stable basis for identity or self-acceptance—the fact that God created us and loves us. He loves us even though he, more than anyone else, knows our flaws. God used the prophet Isaiah to make it clear to the children of Israel that they had not been forgotten by God even though they were sinful. "Remember these things, O Jacob, for you are my servant, O Israel. I have made you, you are my servant; O Israel, I will not forget you. I have swept away your offenses like a cloud, your sins like the morning mist. Return to me, for I have redeemed you" (Is 44:21-22). If God made us and remembers us, as the Bible declares, then it makes sense to believe he can help us realize who we are and what we are worth.

Strange as it may seem, I have found that the more people worship themselves, the harder it is for them to know who they are. On the other hand, when they begin to worship the Creator, they feel a lot more certain about themselves, his creation.

Resolving the Crisis

To deal with the problems related to identity and self-acceptance, several basic issues need to be understood. First, identity is something you have, not something you find. I have worked with a number of people who approach life as though they were suffering from amnesia. They continually ask others to tell them who they are. Unlike amnesia victims, however, they can remember their past and they have identification. But they are unable to take a good look at themselves and say, "That is me— whether I like me or not, this is me."

I often ask people who are struggling with identity to do a personal inventory. "Take a piece of paper," I say, "and begin to write down what you know about yourself. It helps to start with descriptive statements such as 'I am tall' or 'I am dark complected.' Try to describe yourself emotionally, socially and spiritually as well as physically." You may want to take your own personal inventory before reading further in this book.

Another helpful way to inventory yourself is to write down what you like and dislike. Do you like abstract art? Do you like daisies? How about rhubarb pie? What do you dislike? Rain? Snow? Nosy people? Your likes and dislikes are neither good nor bad in themselves—they are simply you.

As you go through the inventory process, you may begin to realize that you have an identity. You are the dynamic sum of all your characteristics. You are not waiting to happen. You are already here. You may not like all you have found in the inventory, but that is not really the issue. The important thing is that *you can know who you are and then go on from there.*

A second step toward resolving an identity crisis is to realize that it is OK to be who you are right now. This is not to say that you have to like everything you see in yourself. It just means you can accept who you see—the whole package, not each individual detail—as a good person to be.

I was amazed the first time I heard one of my sons refer to himself as a loser. I had never thought of him that way, and I could hardly believe my ears. As I questioned him, I realized he had developed this view from a few isolated failures. Unfortunately his disappointment over some failures had caused him to blot out the success experiences he had also had. He was in danger of accepting a negative identity and then rejecting himself. I began to dispute his view, helping him accept himself as a good person even though he was not perfect. Thanks to God's help and that of some competent teachers and coaches he now can say, "I'm OK!"

If we can't start with the raw materials God has given us, then we have no starting place. This is why labeling people is so destructive. Once we are given a label, we tend to see ourselves only in terms of that label. This can make us lose hope because it leaves us no place to grow. If someone calls me a dummy and I accept the label, there is little I can do about it but be dumb. On the other hand, if I see myself as a worthwhile person who sometimes does dumb things, I can work to correct my errors. We all need help to tell ourselves the truth. Labels never tell the whole truth. I may disappoint myself, but that doesn't invalidate me as a person.

A third step in resolving the identity crisis is to realize that we are capable of growth. It is most difficult to accept ourselves for who we are when we feel we are a dead-end street. Carl Rogers made a major contribution to the lives of hundreds of thousands of people with his book *On Becoming a Person*.[3] In this book he affirms that men and women have a tremendous capacity for growth and change, and it is this capacity for growth that gives real zest to life. Although some of Rogers' views are not consistent with Scripture, the notion of growth certainly is. We are admonished to "grow in the grace and knowledge of our Lord and Savior Jesus Christ" (2 Pet 3:18).

The seventies saw the beginning of the human potential or growth movement. The message rang out loud and clear: "You can be who you want to be." In their book, *Your Perfect Right*, a classic in growth-movement literature, Alberti and Emmons speak out strongly in favor of individual growth in assertiveness. They write:

> The message is clear. Our cultural orientation to the development of appropriately assertive behavior is inadequate. We must begin to value and reward the assertions of each individual, acknowledging the right of self-expression without fear or guilt, valuing the right to an opinion, and recognizing the unique contribution of each person.[4]

Assertiveness training, like other aspects of the growth movement, found immediate popularity because it helped people see that personal change is possible. As people realized they could grow and change they found it easier to accept themselves as they were, because they could look forward to becoming who they wanted to be.

This approach was criticized by many Christians because it left God out of the process. Some argued that it contributed to the development of me-ism, which affirms that I am the most important thing in the universe. But me-ism is not a new disease. Mankind has always been forced to decide, "Am I going to include God in my life or not?" "Am I going to accept God as the source of my identity, or am I going to base my identity on personal growth or accomplishments?" Just because some people base growth on self-worship is no reason for Christians to reject growth altogether. Christians need to have an identity, and they need to grow.

The foundational question is this: Upon what am I going to choose to build my life? I contend that a choice to build one's life upon growth potential apart from God is extremely limiting. I believe Bruce Narramore is right when he states:

This is one truth we can know. We can build our lives around the fact that God is God; what He promised, He will do. From this foundation, we can erect a strong and stable sense of personal identity. Our self-image does not have to rest on the shifting sand of our performance and it does not have to rely on the judgments and evaluations we receive from others. God takes care of the needs that arise from our self-concept.[5]

God is interested in our growth because as we change and grow we come closer to being the people he intends us to be. In true fatherly fashion he watches with pride as we grow physically, emotionally, socially and spiritually.

Personal Identity and Other People

Resolving the identity crisis is also aided by good relations with a wide range of people. Identity is affirmed in sound relationships. Unfortunately a person struggling with identity tends to withdraw from people instead of turning to them as a means of support. Jackie said to me, "I just don't know who I am anymore." When I asked her whom she was talking to about her situation she said, "No one! I'm just too embarrassed to have anyone know what kind of mess I'm in."

When he was on earth in bodily form, Jesus had a remarkable way of helping people deal with identity issues. He asked questions like, "Who do men say that I am?" This forced his disciples to think not only about his identity, but their own as well. The New Testament accounts of Jesus with his disciples and close friends reveal a small group of people who serve as a sounding board for each other so they can learn more about themselves. This created conflict whenever the disciples began to make comparisons. Peter fell into this trap, and Jesus forcefully but gently brought him back into line. Notice John 21:21-22: "When Peter saw him, he asked, 'Lord, what about him?' Jesus answered, 'If I want him to remain alive until I return, what is that to you? You must follow me.' "

Small groups can be vital to developing identity, but care must be taken so that the group does not stifle the uniqueness of its members. Comparing and competing don't resolve identity crises. What results is other-directed people who do not know who they are. Groups may also stifle resolution of identity crises if they try to make everyone think and behave the same. God did not create us to all be alike. He created us as individuals. We are alike only in that we are created in his image; how we reflect that image is up to us. Group members may be like-minded, but they lose their identity if they become clones. Among the disciples Jesus chose, there is tremendous diversity. Their differences helped them discover their uniqueness.

When Sally and Tom first joined a small group of couples at their church, they were excited. For the first time in their lives they were going to have Christian friends. But after a few group meetings, their excitement began to wane. They had expected the other couples to be more like them. Tom was disappointed to discover that he was the only male in the group who liked concerts more than ball games. Sally struggled with the fact that her political views differed from those of her newfound friends. Sally and Tom almost dropped out. Tom said, "I don't know whether it's worth it. I just can't be like them."

Fortunately they decided that before they did anything they would talk to Jim and Sue, the leaders of the group. Jim and Sue identified with their concerns and suggested that they stay in the group, not to become like the others but just to be themselves. They were encouraged when Jim said, "We need your perspective." The group began helping Sally and Tom to confirm and strengthen their individual identities by allowing them to be who they are. If it had tried to force them into a mold, it would have stifled their growth and created identity confusion.

People who seem to know who they are usually have a strong sense of commitment. Identity and purpose in life seem to go together. People caught in an identity crisis do not have purpose. One young man said, "If I knew what I was meant to be, I might not feel so bad."

One explanation for the growth of some religious cults is that they provide people with a sense of purpose. They place heavy demands on people in terms of commitment, but they also provide strong group support. Recently as I sat in the Portland Airport watching hundreds of followers of Bhagwan Shree Rajneesh milling about, I wondered about their identity conflicts. They were obviously committed—they were all in uniform. They were also all speaking the party line ("How wonderful it is when you find the Buddha or the Christ within"). They talked individually, but dressed and acted collectively. I wondered what kind of identity these young people will have ten or twenty years from now.

I was impressed by the contrast between this group and many groups of Christians. Both ask for strong commitment. Both offer a purpose in life. The major difference is that a commitment to Jesus Christ is an opportunity to develop your individuality for the sake of the group rather than a demand to sacrifice your individuality to show you are part of the group.

Freedom and Responsibility

Christianity and the cults show great differences in their approaches on freedom and responsibility. Some say that Christianity allows too much individuality and therefore has not become the continually strong social force it could be. I disagree. Individual freedom, properly applied, is one of the hallmarks of Christianity and a source of its strength. The Greek words *eleutheria* and *eleutheros*, "unrestrained, at liberty, not a slave," are used over twenty-five times in the New Testament. John 8:32 states that it is truth which sets us at liberty and frees us from sin. "Then you will know the truth, and the truth will set you free." This theme is continued in Romans 6, and a new twist is added: "You have been set free from sin and have become slaves to righteousness" (Rom 6:18).

What does it mean to be slaves of righteousness? How do freedom and slavery relate to identity? Romans 6:19 clarifies these issues: "I put this in human terms because you are weak in your natural selves. Just as you used to offer the parts of your body in slavery to impurity and to ever-increasing wickedness, so now offer them in slavery to righteousness leading to holiness." When you are freed from sin, this passage says, you are then free to live out God's purpose for you. This is ultimate freedom. It is not freedom to be a robot or a clone; it is freedom to be an individual. Christians give up this freedom if they define Christianity so narrowly that it stamps out individuality or if they return to the lifestyle of the world which is still enslaved by sin. Galatians 5:1 issues a strong warning: "It is for freedom that Christ has set us free. Stand firm, then, and do not let yourselves be burdened again by a yoke of slavery."

Christianity offers both freedom and purpose—freedom to grow as an individual and the dual purpose of serving God with your life and helping others find the individual freedom they seek. This is a distinct challenge which requires more than putting on a red shirt or talking the party line.

What about responsibility? I believe Christianity is unique in that it stresses both group and individual responsibility. I cannot be a responsible Christian and give up my individuality. God has created me as an individual, and he expects me to take that responsibility seriously. But he also calls me to show responsibility to the group—by exercising my individual gifts and by being willing as the need arises to submit myself to others. This is different from abandoning my individuality. The more I am fully me, the more I can be fully a part of a group. In like manner, the more I have a purpose for living, the more I will understand who I am.

Awareness of purpose usually accomplishes two things: It promotes growth in self-acceptance, and it usually also encourages humility. The more I become aware of my purpose in life, the more I realize that it is OK to be me. If I have a purpose as I am, then why not be who I am? On the other hand, the larger the purpose I serve, the more I realize my inadequacies. When

I recognize that I am inadequate I may respond in one of two ways: I can withdraw from the purpose, or I can trust God to enhance my capabilities. Trusting God enables me to grow.

In God's plan, humility leads to faith which leads to growth which leads to greater humility. Humility is not the absence of self-esteem. Humility is recognizing that God is equipping us for all aspects of life. Humility is willingness to accept life as it is and to trust God to help us live it to the fullest. It is a choice to be who we are. A humble person does not let fear push him into being less than he is. Neither does he let pride say that he must be greater before he will recognize his worth.

Jesus, our example of humility, lived out his purpose as a human being. The fact that he was also God did not hinder him from accepting his full identity as a man. He knew who he was. Even though he did not like the abuse he suffered, he refused to be less than the total person he was. Notice carefully these statements from Philippians 2:8-11:

And being found in appearance as a man, *he humbled himself* and became obedient to death—even death on a cross! Therefore *God exalted him* to the highest place and gave him the name that is above every name, that at the name of Jesus every knee should bow, in heaven and on earth and under the earth, and every tongue confess that Jesus Christ is Lord, to the glory of God the Father [emphasis added].

Humility is not self-rejection; it is the highest form of self-acceptance. It is willingness to be who we are and to fulfill the purposes God places in front of us.

When I lived in Iran I often saw devout Muslims flagellating themselves during holy days. This brutal attempt to demonstrate humility and to gain favor with God stands in direct contrast to what I believe God has in mind for Christians. We are to demonstrate our humility by being who we are, not by injuring ourselves. The only blood God takes pleasure in is the blood of Christ, which was shed for us. We dare not turn our attempts to show humility into a self-centered religious custom.

Is there such a thing as an identity crisis? Yes, there is. It is not, however, the problem of who we are. It is the problem of being who we are. It is not "Who am I?" but rather "How can I be who I am?"

The basis for resolving the identity crisis is to recognize that our basic identity comes from God. We have worth because he says we have worth. When we recognize this, we are free to live out our purpose, to be affirmed in relationships, and to live humbly without physical or psychological self-destruction.

3
Basic Components of Identity

IF YOU LOOK AT identity struggles over the past three decades, you will see that about every ten years a new question is asked. In the sixties the question was clearly, "Who am I?" This search for self-knowledge was coupled with a strong emphasis on social concerns. Young people moved away from the established monetary success orientation of the fifties. Students marched to Mississippi to register voters; they swarmed into the ghettos to tutor young children from other ethnic groups; and they rushed to the aid of the elderly. They sensed that personal identity was to be found in serving others. They answered the question "Who am I?" in part by saying, "I am the one who is concerned. I am the one who can serve. I can make a difference."

During the seventies it became more and more difficult to find young people committed to helping others. I was assigned to recruit volunteers to help people with emotional difficulties, and it became difficult if not impossible to find willing workers during this time. Other volunteer programs also went begging. People learned to be self-protective. Their goal was whatever they wanted to do for themselves. The charisma of serving seemed lost. Sparked by dismay over the Vietnam war, people invested their efforts in looking out for themselves even if they were not sure what they wanted. Interest in serving others declined; fulfillment seemed to be the order of the day. Drugs became a way of life for many. The Jesus movement died down as students and other young adults turned their energies to a nondirected search for personal growth.

As the eighties approached and the economy became less dependable, there seemed to be a resurgence of interest in traditional values. Students have begun to look again at three-piece suits and to see value in a good job. Corporate recruiters are once again welcome on campus. Issues from past decades remain, but they are overwhelmed by current economic woes. Without money and without jobs, young people are forced to live at home instead of in their own apartments. They are also faced with the prospect that their hard-earned college degree may not be worth the paper it is printed on. The ideological battle lines of the eighties seem to be drawn between the haves and the have-nots. When the economy is weak, people are primarily concerned with survival. This too has an effect on identity as people jostle in line to receive surplus food or to compete for a limited number of jobs. Competition is inevitable between males and females, Black and White, old and young.

The seventies and the eighties produced a new type of scholar called a futurist. The crisis of the nineties may very well be based not on "Who am I?" but on "Will I have a future? What is in store for me if I survive?"

What does all this have to do with identity and self-acceptance? I believe the answer is clear: identity is not formed in a vacuum. We are products of our culture, and to understand ourselves we have to understand the world in which we live. How important are social concerns to who you are? What impact has the self cult had on you? Are you your own God?

Today we all must face life under the threat of nuclear war and poverty. How does this affect our self-image? If there is a future, will we be ready for it? Many people are extremely frightened by a world of computers and genetic engineering. Is there room for the individual in that type of society? These are the questions feeding into the modern identity crisis. They must be answered individually but no one dares ignore them.

With all the dramatic changes in our society, we have to ask if anything consistent can be used to measure the person. Does personal identity go beyond cultural constraints? I believe it does. I believe man has been programmed so that living above the circumstances is possible. Man has basic needs which must be met regardless of the cultural emphasis of the day. This creates a constant tension point, because leaders in each decade imply that the issue of the day is the issue for all times. The implication is that if we get on board we will know ourselves. There seems to be no place for individual differences. If we want to be important, we have to do what the culture says is important.

The Anchor-Point

I believe we can go beyond the dictates and constraints of culture to experience our true identity. We are not created by culture; we are created by God and then influenced by culture. The Bible makes it clear that God knows us as his creation:

Where can I go from your Spirit? Where can I flee from your presence? If I go up to the heavens, you are there; if I make my bed in the depths, you are there. If I rise on the wings of the dawn, if I settle on the far side of the sea, even there your hand will guide me, your right hand will hold me fast. For you created my inmost being; you knit me together in my mother's womb. (Ps 139:7-10, 13)

Knowing that we are created by and known by God allows us to stop floating in the cosmos. If we are known, then we have a point to anchor to. We can use the anchor-point, "I am known and accepted by God," as a base from which to explore our potential.

This has several important implications. First, if we are known and accepted by God, *we can accept our total selves.* This is not to say that God accepts our sin; it means rather that he accepts us as sinners and stands ready and willing to forgive our sins. "If you, O LORD, kept a record of sins, O Lord, who could stand? But with you there is forgiveness; therefore you are feared" (Ps 130:3-4).

God's forgiveness and acceptance is an anchor-point for resolving the identity crisis because it gives us a place to go. Without forgiveness life is a dead-end street. Regardless of the path we take, we always end up at a place in our lives from which there is no place to go. We are locked in by our sin and our human limitations. God opens the door and ushers us into new, often unexplored, territory. Who am I? I am an explorer. I am free to make an impact upon my world. I have been given not only the opportunity, but also the responsibility to make a difference. Because God frees me from the limitations of my sin, I am up to the task—not fully prepared, but ready to be prepared as I go along.

Second, if we are known and accepted by God, *we are free to grow.* Physical growth we understand. It is genetically programmed. Babies don't stay babies; they grow up to be men and women. Jean Piaget and other developmental psychologists have helped us understand intellectual growth. It is exciting to see people mature mentally from being completely concrete in their thinking to being able to handle abstract thought. Emotional and social growth are no less miraculous. I believe one reason Jesus loved to hold children on his lap was that he saw their great growth potential and was excited about who they were becoming.

Third, if we are known and accepted by God, *we can set goals.* Identity is never fully realized until we have a direction for our lives. It takes courage to set goals in an uncertain world. The more uncertain the world seems, the less willing people are to set goals. Many times when I have asked college students about their goals for the future they have replied, "What future? I don't know that there will be a future." In contrast to this pessimistic view, Scripture strongly emphasizes the presence of God with us in the future regardless of circumstances. "For this God is our God for ever and ever; he will be our guide even to the end" (Ps 48:14). This same emphasis is carried forward in the New Testament. The writer of Hebrews stated: "Let us hold unswervingly to the hope we profess, for he who promised is faithful. And let us consider how we may spur one another on toward love and good deeds" (Heb 10:23-24). Considering "how we may spur one another on toward love and good deeds" is obviously compatible with goal setting. We are able to set goals because we have hope. Once again God is the anchor-point from which we move out to be who he created us to be.

Identity and Personality Structure

It is not enough just to say that our identity is anchored in God. We still have to live our lives and become our own persons. God lives within believers, but he chooses to enhance individual personality rather than supersede it.

In *The Undivided Self,* I suggested that personality can be viewed as having four basic components: thinking, feeling, choosing and doing. If any one of these components is missing, we are not complete. We think. We feel. We act. We make decisions. That is what being human is all about.

I have found that if a person is weak in any one of these areas, his or her identity may be strongly affected. Martin is a good example. He appears to have it all together. He is bright. In fact he is so bright that he intimidates people. He is a decision maker, at least in the business area. He gets things done. What about feelings? Martin doesn't allow himself to feel. When pressed, he says, "I'm no mush head. I just deal with facts." The closer you get to Martin, the more you become aware that something is wrong. When he is away from his desk and other symbols of power, Martin is tentative and uncertain. When one of his employees cries, he can't handle it. When Martin faces decisions that touch on feelings, he becomes ineffective because he has walled off all his feelings. His friends wonder what is wrong with Martin.

Jim's identity has also been affected by a lack in one aspect of his personality. He is a good thinker, he is in touch with his emotions, and he gets things done. The problems come to light in the area of choice. Jim suffers from indecisiveness. Jim is afraid of making mistakes, so he has trouble making decisions. This causes him tremendous pain. When he can't decide what to do, he feels like a wasted person. "Any real person can make simple decisions," he said with tears in his eyes.

Marlene's problem is in the area of doing. "I'm not dependable," she said. "I talk a good game, but when it comes right down to it I'm not worth much. I can tell you what I should do but I just don't get things done." Marlene lacks the skill to follow through.

Dave's weakness is in the thinking area. Dave said, "I'm bright, but I'm not very smart." He is uncommitted and unpredictable, because he has not formed the habit of thinking things through. "I don't know who I am," he said, "because my thoughts go in so many directions." Other people don't know who Dave is either. Dave started college believing in complete open-mindedness. He poured more and more ideas into his mind until he didn't know what to think or believe. The more confused he became, the more he looked for new ideas.

Martin, Jim, Marlene and Dave all were weak in one personality area, and all suffered from a lack of self-acceptance and a fuzzy identity. Dave's story, however, has a happy ending. One day he said, "I've come to the place where I believe life doesn't have intellectual solutions. The more I try to solve the human puzzle, the more confused I become. I think my pastor is right. I need to go back to basics." For Dave this meant committing himself to a body of belief around which he could organize his life. He began to study Scripture on his own and to learn all he could about Jesus. The more he became aware of the consistency of Scripture and the uniqueness of the life of Jesus, the more content he became. He still has intellectual questions, but he is no longer "always learning but never able to acknowledge the truth" (2 Tim 3:7). Dave has become a committed believer.

Os Guinness writes, "The biblical view of knowledge has many dimensions, some of which go far beyond a knowing which is solely related to reasons, but "reason-able" knowledge is a basic part of knowing in the Bible. Biblically, much of what is knowable can be checked, verified, substantiated and confirmed."[1] The intellectual and emotional confirmation of the truth of the gospel gave Dave a basis for accepting himself.

Self-Acceptance and Others

God created people to need each other. God saw that "it is not good for the man to be alone" (Gen 2:18). I sometimes wonder, however, if he ever feels some of us overdo it. Many people cannot stand to be alone for even a few short hours. They quickly become fearful and unsure of what might happen to them. Other people interact with others strictly to build up their own ego. They can accept themselves only when they feel accepted by others. Identity for them is found in other people. But this can cause serious problems. We cannot rely on the opinions of others for our identity. People are too fickle. They will let you down and misinterpret your true value to build themselves up. This is why I stress that our identity must be anchored in God. Once the anchor is in place, however, social interaction can play a valuable role in developing self-acceptance.

Our involvement with others can foster self-acceptance in four major ways. First, we feel accepted as we realize we have something to give others. The Bible calls this becoming a servant. Jesus said, "He who is least among you all—he is the greatest" (Lk 9:48). I believe Jesus was calling attention not only to the need for a spirit of servanthood but also to the positive effects serving others has on our own self-acceptance. The key, of course, is to serve others without having to be the greatest servant. Even servanthood can become dangerously competitive!

Second, our self-acceptance increases as we are affirmed by others. Kay often says to Sandy and me, "You have great value to me. You are being used by God in my life. You challenge me to grow." Hearing this certainly doesn't hurt our self-acceptance. We are not responsible for Kay's personal and spiritual growth, and we know God is using others in her life too, but it is nice that she tells us we have value to her. We often have the misguided concept that we harm people when we affirm them. We think we will hurt their humility. This is a real trap. People need to be told they have value. Too often we only tell them what they do wrong. If there is a problem with humility, God will take care of it. Our job is to give encouragement.

Third, our self-acceptance increases as others provide an atmosphere in which self-awareness can grow. The more I am with other people, the more I learn about myself. If I remain open to seeing myself as others see me, I will be both affirmed and challenged—affirmed in my gifts and challenged to develop my potential and correct my shortcomings.

When Dick first joined our small group he was constantly questioning his worth. He wanted to be valuable to God and to the group, but he couldn't seem to figure out how. The more he interacted with the group, the more the group helped him define himself. He began to risk using the gifts God had given him. As he did so, he was affirmed. He traded in "the blues" for an upward spiral of personal growth. It is not hard to want to grow or to correct a fault when we know we have a group of loving people behind us. On the other hand, growth in isolation is almost impossible. Hebrews 10:24-25 makes this clear: "Let us consider how we may spur one another on toward love and good deeds. Let us not give up meeting together, as some are in the habit of doing, but let us encourage one another—and all the more as you see the Day approaching."

Last, others can help us see a vision of who God wants us to be. I would never have written a book if it were not for the strong support I received from my wife and members of our small group. They challenged me both to be and to do. Writing or singing or preaching or teaching does not make me great. It may, however, provide me with the outlet I need to express who God has made me to be. When I am who God intended, self-acceptance is easier.

The Journey

Identity and self-acceptance grow by stages that we must understand. I like to look at these stages as a journey. We begin the journey lost at sea. Some people drift aimlessly for years. Others realize that their compass points to God. Keeping their sights trained on him, they know they have worth because he made them and values them. The next step in the journey is to realize that God has given us the tools for navigation: the mind, the emotions, choices and actions.

Our journey is enriched by the other ships we meet. It's comforting to be able to see the lights of the other vessels, especially when the water gets rough.

4
Steps to Understanding Me

MUCH OF THE CONFUSION people face in dealing with problems of self-worth comes from a basic lack of self-understanding.
Through helping people deal with this issue, I have discovered
several steps to overcome this deficiency.

The Blessings of Complexity
Human beings are highly complex. The psalmist had this in
mind when he wrote, "I praise you because I am fearfully and
wonderfully made; your works are wonderful, I know that full
well" (Ps 139:14). Complexity is a blessing, but at times we may
wish we were less complex so we could understand ourselves
better. As Jim said, "Why can't I just take things in stride? I
always have to do things the hard way."

Have you ever wished you were a robot? Robots do only what

they are programmed to do. In one sense we are programmed too—we are designed to love God and our fellow man, and we are designed to serve God and others. The problem is that God wants our service and love to be voluntary, and he thus allows us to override the existing program.

Our freedom creates emotional and intellectual conflicts. Our motives get confused and we sometimes act in ways that seem foreign to us. One reason the teen years are so volatile is that during adolescence, the person is growing more complex mentally, physically, emotionally and socially. Yet complexity is not a curse. It is a sign of opportunity. The more complex the organism, the more freely it can choose what kind of life it will have.

When you find yourself confused by your complexity, don't try to solve the riddle too quickly. Stand back and look at yourself. Don't panic; just relax and allow yourself to see what you can see. Even when you are looking at yourself, you can realize that God is more complex than you are. He wants you to get to know him. The psalmist David wrote, "Be still, and know that I am God" (Ps 46:10). It is comforting to know that God wants you to increase your self-understanding as well as your knowledge of him.

Feelings: Our Vital Signs

Have you ever touched a feeling? They may be warm and soft on one side and cold and prickly on the other. Feelings change rapidly, like characters in video games. Now you see them; now you don't. Feelings touch every aspect of you. People who deny their feelings do not really understand themselves. For example, if I refuse to admit to my anger, I may wonder why I am so tired all the time. Keeping anger suppressed is hard work. On the other hand, if I fail to recognize my feelings of love for the young woman in my English literature class, I may not know why I always get to that class on time when I am late for most of my other classes.

Sometimes I don't know I am afraid until I catch myself shaking. I could often avoid embarrassment and failure if I just knew earlier what was happening inside me. The signals are usually there, but I choose to ignore them because I *shouldn't* have fears. The truth is, fears control a great deal of my life as they do anybody's. If we don't understand this fact, we may pay by losing self-esteem.

A forty-year-old client had never admitted that he had a high need for acceptance. Thus when Jerry felt rejected he could not talk to his family about it. Instead, he withdrew from the stage where acceptance was playing. Resentments grew, and, as he said, "things began to come out sideways." He began violating his standards to make himself feel better. The result was a further loss of acceptance, ending in the loss of the most important acceptance of all—acceptance of self. When he began to acknowledge this emotional need, Jerry learned to move toward people when acceptance was in short supply. This helped him break the downward spiral of self-pity, withdrawal, inappropriate behavior, guilt and self-rejection.

Feelings are our vital signs. They usually tell us when something is needed or when something is wrong. Unfortunately many of us believe that feelings are bad. This is not true. Without feelings we would be like rocks or trees. With feelings we can learn what it means to be created in God's image. Just because feelings cause difficulty doesn't mean we need to amputate them. Once we understand them, they become valuable. We have to choose how to respond to our feelings, but such choices help us understand who we really are.

Recognizing Presuppositions

If you are old enough to read this book, you do not have an open mind. Each of us has grown up with beliefs and presuppositions that have a marked effect on the way we think and solve problems. Because we cannot understand ourselves without understanding our thoughts, it is crucial to understand those presuppositions. They affect all that we do, say and think.

In *The Universe Next Door,* James Sire discusses world views which shape our thinking. He writes:

Few people have anything approaching an articulate philosophy—at least as epitomized by the great philosophers. Even fewer, I suspect, have a carefully constructed theology. But everyone has a world view. Whenever any of us thinks about anything—from a casual thought (Where did I leave my watch?) to a profound question (Who am I?)—we are operating within such a framework. In fact, it is only the assumption of a world view—however basic or simple—that allows us to think at all.

"What, then, is this thing called a world view that is so important to all of us? I've never even heard of one. How could I have one?" . . . To discover one's own world view . . . is a significant step toward self-awareness, self-knowledge and self-understanding.[1]

I encourage you to study your philosophical assumptions carefully to increase your self-awareness.

Psychological presuppositions may also strongly affect self-understanding. Donna may have a presupposition that says, "I have to be loved and approved of by everybody." This may explain why she wastes so much time and energy worrying about what people think about her. This presupposition tends to destroy self-acceptance, because even if she were perfectly lovable, somebody out there wouldn't like her, and this would cause great distress. It is usually healthy to want people to like us, but it can be very destructive if we feel we are worthless unless people approve.

Another destructive presupposition is believing I have to be perfect to be worthwhile. Am I satisfied when I do a good job, or do I continually goad myself to be perfect? Perfectionism is a terrible trap because if I feel I can't do something perfectly, I may not do it at all. Then my guilt will increase, and my confidence will hit a new low. John was almost immobilized by the time we first met. He suffered from this problem largely because his parents had never told him when he had done a good job. They always reminded him when he wasn't perfect, however. Unfortunately he was painfully aware of his imperfections already. I asked him to set goals or performance levels which, if reached, would allow him to feel good about himself. As he reached goal after goal, his self-acceptance began to rise. It was a long emotional struggle before the old habits began to break, but today he would tell you it was worth it all.

Defeatism may also be a controlling presupposition. I have met many students who believe they can't do anything hard. Consequently, their world of possibilities grows smaller and smaller. "I can't do it! It is just too hard," Margaret cried. Her friends, able to see much of her natural ability, knew she had resources she hadn't begun to tap. Unfortunately, however, her defeatism dammed up her resources. It took some supportive friends and a persistent teacher who believed in Margaret to get her to take steps toward doing difficult things. Her response to her first success was typical. "Wow," she said, "if I had known it was that easy, I would have tried it a lot sooner."

God made life to be challenging so we can grow. It can be healthy to say, "I don't know whether I'm going to do well or badly, but I'm going to give the situation my best effort." When we do this, we shouldn't expect perfection but we should expect success. With a victory, this crippling presupposition will begin to crumble.

Have you ever said, "That's not fair"? If so, you may have the presupposition that people should treat you fairly. This presupposition is damaging because life is not fair, and if you expect fairness you may end up rejecting yourself as unworthy of fair treatment. Once Mike learned to accept unfairness as a consequence of living in a sinful world, he was able to approach unfair situations much more positively. He learned that life isn't fair but that he could do his part to make it fairer. He began to challenge unfairness when he could and accept it as reality when he couldn't. This enabled him to quit feeling sorry for himself.

Boredom is also usually anchored in an unhealthy presupposition that I should always be happy, interested or excited. Impossible! If I were excited all the time, my body wouldn't know how to handle the chemical overload. I need highs, but I also need lows to give me a chance to recuperate and prepare for new experiences. I have to face it: life is going to be boring much of the time. I will find my self-acceptance increasing as I learn to accept boredom while looking for creative ways to challenge it.

Paul Hauck writes:

The person who cannot tolerate boredom never plows through the muck of hard work which is necessary to reach the higher and more interesting levels of achievement. Instead, when he gets stuck in boredom he turns around and tries another approach to the mountaintop—and runs into another swamp. He goes back and forth around the base of the mountain trying to cross the swamps and never gets to where he wants to go. The trouble with people who stop at the boredom phase is that they think boredom is *terrible*.[2]

It takes a creative person to persist long enough to climb to the top of a mountain, especially if he or she doesn't like hiking. Bored people don't usually look at the scenery, and thus they remain bored. Bored people also fail to look at their accomplishments, and thus they feel bad about themselves or even deserted by God. I made a great discovery the day I realized I could be bored and happy at the same time.

Thus far all the presuppositions I have mentioned have been negative. They are hindrances to personal health. There are, however, presuppositions which may be positive and productive. Let me mention a few just to whet your appetite. The ones I have selected all have a strong base in Scripture. They are more than just happy thoughts.

God created me and values me. Most Christians believe that they are created by God, but many still find it hard to believe that God places value on them. If he doesn't value us, why does he put up with us? We are not his last hope. But the fact remains that God chose us. We are his loved ones. Scripture says, "You are a chosen people, a royal priesthood, a holy nation, a people belonging to God, that you may declare the praises of him who called you out of darkness into his wonderful light. Once you were not a people, but now you are the people of God; once you had not received mercy, but now you have received mercy" (1 Pet 2:9-10). Why not think of yourself as one of God's special people?

God forgives me and nurtures me. I constantly need forgiveness. Even when I seek diligently to live a good life, I fail. That is hard on my self-esteem until I realize that God not only forgives my failures but also provides me with the nurture I need to go on with life. John 21 shows how forgiveness and nurture go together. Jesus forgave Peter for betraying him, and he nurtured Peter by helping Peter understand that betrayal didn't mean that he didn't love him. It was also nurturing for Peter to remember he was still useful. Jesus said, "Follow me."

God does not take pleasure in our failures. God sent Christ to die for those failures, and now he wants us to focus on him and our future. Why do we believe that God is more interested in our past than our present and our future?

If we claim to be without sin, we deceive ourselves and the truth is not in us. If we confess our sins, he is faithful and just and will forgive us our sins and purify us from all unrighteousness. If we claim we have not sinned, we make him out to be a liar and his word has no place in our lives. My dear children, I write this to you so that you will not sin. But if anybody does sin, we have one who speaks to the Father in our defense—Jesus Christ, the Righteous One. He is the atoning sacrifice for our sins, and not only for ours but also for the sins of the whole world. (1 Jn 1:8—2:2)

The emphasis throughout Scripture is to accept God's forgiveness and get on with living for him. In so doing we will find out who we are and who we can become.

Persons with low self-esteem usually have difficulty believing or accepting emotionally what the Scripture says in passages like Romans 8. We need to learn to believe and feel that *God both equips us and encourages us.* Notice carefully what Scripture says at this point:

In the same way, the Spirit helps us in our weakness. We do not know what we ought to pray, but the Spirit himself intercedes for us with groans that words cannot express. And we know that in all things God works for the good of those who love him, who have been called according to his purpose. What, then, shall we say in response to this? If God is for us, who can be against us? He who did not spare his own Son, but gave him up for us all—how will he not also, along with him, graciously give us all things? (Rom 8:26, 28, 31-32)

When we look for God's influence on our lives, we will find it. When we ask for strength and encouragement, he gives it. The presupposition that God equips and encourages is a key both to living by faith and to understanding our own potential.

Another positive presupposition is that *God understands me and watches over me.* Recently I had one of those days in which I made one error after another. I believe my computer was set on self-destruct. Somehow I didn't panic, and the day did come to an end. As I discussed my perils with my wife that evening, we made some interesting discoveries. First, Sandy's life had also been topsy-turvy. I wasn't alone. God wasn't just picking on me. Second, God had watched over us in such a way that even our blunders were of little consequence. He had not forgotten us. We savored that fact together. Both of us decided we could face a new day with such an understanding God. Psalm 23 is not just a pretty poem. It is God's promise of watchfulness. Likewise Psalm 139 gives strong assurance of God's understanding. "O LORD, you have searched me and you know me. You know when I sit and when I rise; you perceive my thoughts from afar. You discern my going out and my lying down; you are familiar with all my ways. Before a word is on my tongue you know it completely, O LORD. You hem me in, behind and before; you have laid your hand upon me. Such knowledge is too wonderful for me, too lofty for me to attain" (Ps 139:1-6).

When our presuppositions are based on Scripture, our self-confidence will rise. We will come to understand that God values us because of who we are and what we can do with our lives.

Checking Our Tracks

One of the best barometers for understanding ourselves is our behavior. We are to a large degree the sum of our actions. Motives and intentions do matter. But if we really want to know who we are, we should spend more time looking at what we did and less time musing over what we intended to do. The apostle James supports this: "Do not merely listen to the word, and so deceive yourselves. Do what it says. Anyone who listens to the word but does not do what it says is like a man who looks at his face in a mirror and, after looking at himself, goes away and immediately forgets what he looks like" (Jas 1:22-24).

When I compare my intentions with my actual behavior I often have reason for remorse. There may be many reasons for my shortcomings, but the bottom line is this: the way I behave affects the person I become.

A helpful way to increase self-understanding is to look at the relative strength of some of my contradictory behavior. If, for example, I say that I am devoted to my family, I need to compare the amount of time I spend with my wife and children with the time I spend with friends or at work. If the balance is really tilted toward friends or work, I need to come to grips with the fact that I am more devoted to friends and work than to my family. Facing such truths is not easy, but it is essential if I am going to understand myself.

If your boyfriend, girlfriend or spouse tells you that he or she loves you but does not choose to spend time with you, then you need to seriously face the fact that love for you is not a predominant factor in his or her life. You can analyze your own personality from a behavioral perspective also. How much time do you spend letting off steam or talking to others about things that make you angry? How much time do you spend withdrawing from people because of fear? How much time do you spend singing? Expressing emotions is like using a pipeline: the more you do it, the faster the flow. The more joy you express, the more joy you experience. The more depression you act out (by staying in bed, drinking, refusing to eat or withdrawing from friends) the more depressed you feel. Behaving appropriately, even when you don't feel like it, may be a tremendous step toward self-acceptance. Wanda is only seventeen, but she has learned a lot about herself by looking at her behavior. She sees good behavior, so she knows that she can do well. She also sees bad behavior, so she knows the temptation to fall back into some of her negative patterns is still there.

Sometimes when I feel bad or upset or guilty I do not understand why. I may find the answer by looking at my behavior for the last few weeks. This is called "checking my tracks." What have I been doing? Is there any possible connection between what I have done and how I feel at the moment? Often I will find that there is. When I discover the connection, I can take action to make myself feel better. For example, if I remember I have been talking behind a friend's back, I may understand why I am feeling guilty or upset. One experiment I can try is to stop the backbiting and see what happens to my feelings.

Self-discovery can be exciting. Taking the risk of examining our own behavior is often scary, but it gives us more control over our lives and more opportunity to decide how we want to be.

The Importance of Choice

Choice is "the chance, right or power to choose, usually by the free exercise of one's judgment." This definition causes me problems at times, because I am not always willing to acknowledge just how many events in my life result from my free exercise of judgment. I would rather make excuses than say I failed because

I chose to put off doing the required work. The devil-made-me-do-it attitude is so prevalent in our society that we often fail to think about how important our choices can be.

I must take responsibility for three important choices in life: priorities, plan of action and personal style. The first area of choice is priorities. I believe in being proactive, not reactive. To do this, I must decide where to invest my time and energy. Setting priorities is difficult, because there are so many opportunities to choose among. It is easy to forget what I really want out of life. In *Balancing Life's Demands,* Grant Howard writes:

OPTIONS! In the battle of life we are up against options. Everywhere we turn there are choices to be made. Obligations that pressure us. Opportunities that entice us. We are bombarded with places to go, overrun with people to meet, pinned down with things to buy, fatigued with mail to read. We are being inundated on all sides by powerful forces that clamor for our time, talents, money, influence, wisdom. There is also a psychological aspect to this campaign: We are infiltrated by feelings of guilt because we cannot possibly respond to all the options.[3]

An important part of self-understanding is recognizing that we must choose from among the options open to us. Not choosing only amounts to choosing a different path. Are you a chooser, or do you wait for someone else to tell you what to do? I believe that we greatly enhance our self-esteem each time we are willing to decide and then act on our best judgment. I once asked a depressed client if she was having trouble making decisions. She said, "I don't even let myself think of the problems, let alone the decisions that might help solve them." Choice can be freeing. It allows us to set the course for our own ship. But it also requires us to be responsible once we have set our priorities.

The second area of choice, a plan of action, can tell us a lot about ourselves. When we drive cross-country, are we likely to take the freeway or the more scenic routes? Why? Analyzing that choice can help us see if we are future- or present-oriented, more concerned with means or with ends. There isn't a right or wrong way to be, but it can help our self-esteem to know how we are. For years one of my friends felt guilty every time he took the longer route to get to his destination. One day he realized, "I like looking at trees or rivers better than cars, and if I make that choice I really don't care if other people are different."

We often mistakenly think that a choice of priorities carries with it a built-in plan of action. Not so! Our choice to serve God doesn't say how we are to serve God. We make that decision according to our abilities, interests and circumstances. The important thing is to *choose* a plan of action. If we wait for others to lead us by the hand, either we will never act or others will choose a plan for us. Either situation can make it hard to accept ourselves.

The third area of choice is personal style. I can choose to marry or to be single, to have children or to remain childless, to broaden my education or to remain specialized. I can choose what to eat for breakfast or to skip breakfast altogether.

I have chosen to wear a beard. I like it. It fits in well with another personal choice I have made, to get up late and rush out of the house to my office. My wife also likes it, so that makes the choice even more desirable. One of my friends had trouble handling my choice. He kept trying to rationalize it for me by saying things like, "I'll bet having a beard really increases your effectiveness with college students." In other words, please tell me you are wearing it for a purpose. I finally said, "Tim, I wear the beard because I like it. It really doesn't help me or hurt me. I just like it." He shook his head and walked away.

Later as we talked I realized he was not used to making choices of personal style. He was used to being told what to do and what not to do. Scripture makes it clear that we are free to make such choices. We must be willing, however, not to choose something if it causes a brother to stumble. See Romans 14:14-15. I have chosen to make that concern for others a part of my personal style.

Try to understand yourself by analyzing the choices you make and the choices you refuse to make. Are there choices you could make which would help you more clearly define yourself or see yourself as a person of greater worth? It is worth looking into.

Living with Ambivalence

When faced with a difficult situation, many of us have said, "I just want it all to go away." Difficulties destroy our mental picture of what the world should be like. We would like it to be all light and roses, but we see darkness and thorns as well. In fact, on almost every turn life presents us with ambivalent situations. I may feel loved by someone, but I also feel his or her lack of love. I may be excited about a job interview, but I am also fearful. Ambivalence is an unavoidable part of living in a sinful world. Nothing is perfect; understanding this makes it much easier to not get dragged down by it.

Nancy couldn't accept her feelings of ambivalence and was always trying to make them go away. When she was feeling justifiable anger toward someone she loved, she would deny it and cover it up with a syrupy smile. As long as the fake smile covered her face, she never dealt with the issues. Finally her feelings of anger broke through. The problems she had denied now totally consumed her. She said and did things she will probably regret the rest of her life. How much better it would have been if she had recognized and permitted herself to have ambivalent feelings! Then she could have made better choices about how to deal with each of the contrasting aspects of her experience. Denying ambivalence doesn't make it go away. In fact, it is unhealthy not to feel ambivalent about some things. A picture is never all black or all white; if you do not see shades of gray, beware. And yet ambivalence, though healthy and necessary, can be unsettling.

Here are some steps to help deal with it. First, state both sides of the issue as clearly and as fully as possible. I find it helpful to write down what I discover as I analyze the situation.

Second, ask yourself how you are reacting to what you have discovered. Is the ambivalence affecting you negatively? Is it only annoying you, or is it truly hurting you or adversely affecting your relationships with others? Are you exaggerating or minimizing some aspects of the issue? If so, try to get back to the facts of the situation. You don't have to like everything about it, but neither do you have to let the negative aspects control your life.

Third, ask yourself if you can do anything to clear up the ambivalence. Can you change anything about the situation? Remember, you can't change other people. You can only change yourself. If the ambivalence stems from a conflict in a relationship, ask yourself if you have really tried to hear the other person's point of view or to tell him or her how you feel about the situation.

Fourth, when you understand the situation as well as you can and have done all you can do for the moment, relax and watch what happens. Things may change. If they do, you need to be ready to enjoy the change. Don't let fear of the darkness keep you from seeing the first rays of dawn.

Finally, remind yourself that people don't die from ambivalence. Accentuate the positive but remain aware of the negative so you do not overreact.

God understands ambivalence. He sent his Son to die so we might live. Talk to him honestly about your thoughts and feelings. As you pray, look for his guidance at each step.

Becoming Your Own Scientist

One of the most helpful ways to increase self-understanding is to experiment with behavior. If your self-esteem is low, don't just do the old things over and over. Try something new! As you try new approaches to relationships or to problem-solving, evaluate them carefully. Careful observation of your own behavior can greatly increase your options as well as help you avoid approaches that don't work.

Michael Mahoney has outlined a seven-step sequence for scientific problem-solving which he presents in this acrostic:

Specify the general problem
Collect information
Identify causes or patterns
Examine options
Narrow options and experiment
Compare data
Extend, revise or replace[4]

Many people, seeing a list such as this, draw back and do not try to work with their own situation. I challenge you not to withdraw. Understanding yourself is too important to leave to chance. This approach will teach you a lot about your strengths and weaknesses. As you learn, you will have much more control over your life and will find that your level of self-acceptance is rising.

Scripture tells us to examine ourselves. In other words, self-understanding is not just an option; it is a command. Notice these verses: "A man ought to examine himself before he eats of the bread and drinks of the cup" (1 Cor 11:28). "Examine yourselves to see whether you are in the faith; test yourselves. Do you not realize that Christ Jesus is in you—unless, of course, you fail the test?" (2 Cor 13:5). Self-examination is necessary, not only as you prepare for Communion, but also as you prepare for life.

Finally, if you want to understand yourself, don't shut God out. Allow him to examine you. He will help you see your strengths. Too often we are afraid to open up to God because we fear he will point out our weaknesses. What are you afraid of? You already know your weaknesses. You will deal with them better when you also know your strengths. David's prayer can be a model for you to follow. "Vindicate me, O LORD, for I have led a blameless life; I have trusted in the LORD without wavering. Test me, O LORD, and try me, examine my heart and my mind; for your love is ever before me, and I walk continually in your truth" (Ps 26:1-3).

5
Can I Choose Who I Want to Be?

MANY PEOPLE HAVE difficulty with self-acceptance because they feel their lives are out of their hands. Margaret said, "I didn't ask to be brought into this world, and I don't like the results." Dave was calmer, but his feelings ran just as deep. "I feel like there is nothing I can do. I'm stuck in a body I don't like, and the rest of me is not too hot either." Janice was straight to the point: "I sometimes feel life is a cruel hoax."

Both psychology and religion have at times promoted a deterministic and fatalistic view of life. Many of us believe we are trapped or doomed, and we often play the role of the hapless victim for all it's worth.

Obviously genetics and circumstances put limitations on us. People with slow reflexes do not become professional athletes. Those who are colorblind do not become interior decorators.

On the other hand, some people hide behind their backgrounds and refuse to develop the potential they have, irrationally believing they cannot escape the past. If this is true, then they are indeed doomed to misery.

Two key truths counteract this fatalistic view of life. Both have to do with choice. First, Scripture makes it clear that Christ died for our sins to give us new life. This life is not the one we were born into. That life was and is crippled by the effects of sin. Ephesians refers to our natural state as *death*. We are dead in our sins. "As for you, you were dead in your transgressions and sins, in which you used to live. . . . But because of his great love for us, God, who is rich in mercy, made us alive with Christ" (Eph 2:1, 4). Nobody has to stay dead. But it is a choice we have to make. Do I want God as part of my life or not? If I choose him, he gives me new potential. If I reject him or ignore him, all I have is what I was born with.

In 2 Corinthians 5:17, Paul spells out the way this choice affects our potential. Old life is death; new life in Christ is life complete. "Therefore, if anyone is in Christ, he is a new creation; the old has gone, the new has come!" New life means new potential—a time to start over. It is a choice worth considering.

Another truth which counteracts fatalism is this: we are not puppets or creatures of fate. We can and must choose how we are going to live. Some choices, such as a choice to drink heavily, limit our potential; other choices, such as a choice to follow Christ, open up our potential. I say it again—we are not puppets; we have choices to make.

When I first saw Don, he had chosen to seek pleasure. Everything he did was for the sensation he would get. However, Don was beginning to realize that his choices were leading to self-destruction. He liked to use drugs, but found that when he did so his mind became obsessed with uncontrollable sexual thoughts. These thoughts were driving him to take risks which were destroying him physically, relationally and psychologically. He wanted to seek pleasure without hurting himself and others, but by the time he came to see me he was realizing it was impossible. As the Scripture says, "No one can serve two masters. Either he will hate the one and love the other, or he will be devoted to the one and despise the other" (Mt 6:24).

Joshua challenged the children of Israel to "choose for yourselves this day whom you will serve, whether the gods your forefathers served beyond the River, or the gods of the Amorites, in whose land you are living. But as for me and my household, we will serve the LORD" (Josh 24:15).

Choice has a great deal to do with finding identity and learning to accept oneself. Even secular writers underscore this. In *Choosing: A Better Way to Live* Richard Nelson writes, "Living in a world in which we often feel trapped and limited is not healthy for you, for me, or for other living things. It is within our reach to meet our responsibilities and make better choices, create better relationships, and build better lives."[1] But how do we make choices that will promote self-acceptance and self-discovery?

A Road Map
Once when visiting San Francisco I went looking for an address on the other side of town. Unfortunately, I left my map in my hotel room. Each choice I made on the way seemed to lead to dead-end streets or detours. I began to feel bad about myself and angry at the city. "How could such a pretty place be so confusing?" I lamented. Needless to say, by the time I got to my destination I was late and frustrated. The trip would have been much easier if I had only studied the way more carefully. I knew where I was going; I just didn't take time to determine how to get there.

Some people I know haven't even bothered to select a destination. It is difficult to decide who you want to be when you aren't willing to explore possibilities and dreams. When I was a student in Bible School I was trying to decide what to do with my life. Professor Goodrick saw my struggles and moved alongside to help. His question stunned me. "At what age do you expect to be maximally effective?" he asked.

I was twenty at the time, and twenty-one sounded just right. Patience has always been a virtue with me. He said, "What about fifty?" I shuddered! Fifty sounded like rocking chairs and shuffleboard. He said, "OK, how about thirty-five?" I decided not to prolong the bargaining. "All right! You win!" I said.

The relentless professor went on. "If you want to be maximally effective at age thirty-five," he said, "then how are you going to invest the next fifteen years of your life?" That thought was totally foreign to me. I later realized that by asking the question, he was trying to force me to design a road map to guide my career and educational choices.

Since that time I have helped dozens of college students decide who they want to be and what interim steps they need to take to get there. I found that many people have never learned to set goals. Some fear failure, and others lack discipline. Regardless of the reason, the outcome is usually the same. People who don't know where they are going often forget who they are. They don't usually have high self-worth, either.

When I first met Dawn, she was engulfed by self-hatred. She never found satisfaction in the things she was doing because they didn't seem to be leading anywhere. She had grown careless in study habits, personal grooming and relationships. Her body was fat, and her spirit was emaciated. The first time I mentioned goals, she turned a pale shade of green. She wasn't ready for anything like that. Later, however, she was able to set some goals. As a result, she began to live again rather than just exist.

Her goals were simple. First, to continue in counseling. (She had a history of dropping out when things became difficult.) Second, to lose thirty pounds. And third, to select a college major and begin to work toward completing it. These goals became the road map that helped her make other choices. With each choice she made, she strengthened her identity and her self-acceptance. Although Dawn continued to dislike herself at times, she noticed she was becoming more positive and less self-derogatory.

Getting to Know Me

What do you mean when you say, "I'm confused"? I usually mean, "I don't understand myself. I have thoughts and feelings that don't fit together. I don't always do what I should."

Making good choices which promote self-worth requires self-awareness. Jim has high moral standards and wants desperately to live up to them. He is often depressed and discouraged, however, because his behavior does not match his beliefs. One day I asked, "Jim, are you aware of how high your need for affection is?" He said, "What do you mean?" I explained that he had a high need to know that people cared about him and wanted to be close to him. Because he was not aware of this strong need, he would often get himself into situations where he became sexually aroused. He then usually acted on his arousal.

I helped him begin to distinguish between the need for affection and the need for sex. As he saw this distinction and began to learn other ways to meet his needs, he began to curtail his promiscuous sexual behavior. He amazed himself one day when he said, "I can say no to sex outside of marriage now that I can receive love and affection with my clothes on."

This new awareness helped Jim coordinate his thoughts, feelings and behaviors. With unity in his personality, he could now make the kinds of choices which increase self-acceptance. I discuss this process of bringing thoughts, feelings and actions together more fully in *The Undivided Self.*[2]

Why do thoughts and feelings often seem to take us in different directions? One answer is that we do not understand either our thoughts or our feelings and thus do not bring them under control. Tom didn't want to smoke pot anymore, because it was ruining his marriage. The problem was that he didn't understand the emotions that compelled him to smoke or the thoughts he used to justify his actions. When we talked, he said he had never made a plan for meeting some of his emotional needs other than through smoking. Instead, he was into a downward spiral which went from boredom to smoking to guilt to more boredom.

"What is the cure for boredom?" I asked. We decided that choosing an activity with a purpose would help. As he did this, his guilt began to decrease. When guilt decreased, there was room for self-esteem to grow. Understanding feelings (boredom) and his thoughts (that smoking pot would relieve boredom) helped him substitute more effective thoughts and actions; this in turn led to more satisfying feelings.

It is important to examine thoughts and beliefs. Not just what we believe about God, but what we believe about ourselves as well. Karen, beautiful at age thirty-three, believed she was part of the "over-the-hill gang." This belief triggered feelings of despair which caused her to lose sight of who she is. When she became aware of her thought, she was able to choose to keep her thoughts more honest. Paul wrote that we are to "take captive every thought" (2 Cor 10:5). In other words, whether in spiritual warfare or in struggles with self-acceptance, we have to control our thinking. The first step in such control is awareness. When Karen became aware of her self-defeating thoughts, she was able to admit that being thirty-three is not the end.

Let me suggest a helpful exercise. Take an hour to brainstorm about your thoughts about yourself. Do you like your personality? Do you feel confident at work? Are you competent in relationships? Next, do the same thing with your feelings. What do you feel? How would you like to feel? Let the list of questions expand—the more you know about yourself, the better choices you will be able to make.

While you are in this introspective mood, do not forget to evaluate your behaviors as well. Do you like your actions? What things would you like to do that you are not doing? Are there skills you would like to acquire? Are there disciplines you would like to keep?

Last, evaluate choices you are currently making. Are the choices in line with your thoughts, feelings and behavior? Are your choices consistent with who you want to be? If not, why not try to bring them into line?

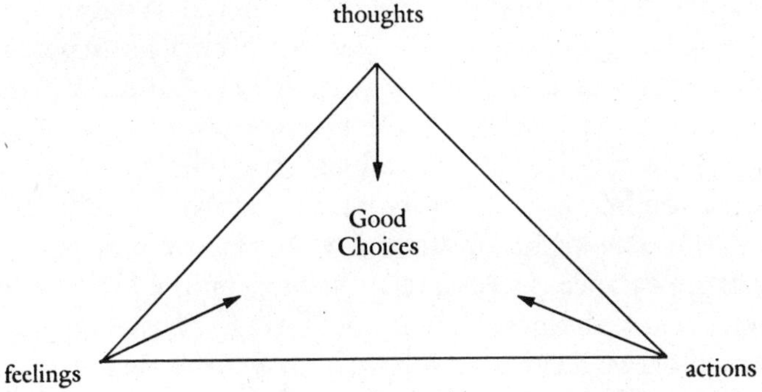

thoughts

Good
Choices

feelings   actions

Figure 1: Choice unifies the person.

Figure 1 points out that good choices bring thoughts, feelings and actions together. This allows self-acceptance to grow. It all begins with awareness. You have to know where you are before you can decide how to get where you want to go.

Turning Loose

My childhood was very happy; I had few disappointments. However, I grew up on a farm, and one thing farm children sometimes have to face more than others is the death of pets. This hit me for the first time when I was nine years old. I sat on the back porch holding the leg of my dead pig. It was cold, almost frozen. I knew my world could never come together again. I felt as cold inside as the leg I held in my hand. My mother and father let me grieve even though they knew I would eventually have to release my dead animal's leg, get up and walk away. They told me that life would go on. Dad said, "You will always remember this pet as special, but you will have others."

Some people hold onto their past like a dead pet. For them the past represents life and identity and worth. They need my father's advice. The past may have been special, but sometimes you have to choose to walk away from the past. What happens to an athlete whose self-worth is tied up in competition if he or she cannot compete at the professional level? What happens to the romantic girl who always wanted to be a housewife if her prince charming leaves her for someone else? If self-worth is to continue, the past must be turned loose.

You may identify with the athlete, the scholar or the housewife, or you may not. But everyone has to turn some things loose to continue his or her journey. Some areas we may need to let go are appearance, success, relationships, failure, death, dreams, hurts, desires, shoulds, should nots, haves or have nots.

Anything we feel we must have in order to be happy may have to be turned loose, at least mentally, if we are to find and accept ourselves. I am not saying we have to turn things loose for the sake of turning them loose. I believe in tenacity! I am saying only that we need to turn loose those things which damage our self-worth. Some people have to let go of self-hatred. Some people have to give up a particular love. The question is, "Does this idea or thing to which I am clinging promote a positive view of myself, or is it tearing me down?" If it is tearing me down I need to turn it loose. This is a deliberate choice.

When Sandy and I were first married, we went to the ocean with my family. While jumping in the waves we discovered that a strong undertow was pulling us out to sea. Both of us were novice swimmers at best. I kept her afloat for a while, but I grew tired as the current became stronger. At one point I even pulled her under. I soon realized I had to turn her loose if either of us was going to survive. Just as I let go, my brother jumped in and pulled her to shore. I rested in the water for a while and then made my own way to the shore.

Turning loose was hard, but it was also the way to life for both of us. What if I had been too stubborn to recognize my own limitations? Stubbornness is a virtue only when coupled with good sense. Invariably choice requires that we give up something. We can't drive as long as we choose to walk. We can't love as long as we refuse to give up hating. What choices are consistent with our growth in self-acceptance? What are we going to have to let go to make those good choices?

Taking Hold

Some people find it easier to give up the past than to take hold of the future. Many of my clients are miserable because of things from the past they are clinging to. They often know what they need to turn loose and what they need to take hold of, but they are unable to do either. Leon said, "I can handle the pain of the past and even the present. What I don't know is whether I can handle the pain that might be associated with the unknown."

My response to him was, "You will never know until you take hold."

Taking hold is difficult because it requires dealing with three kinds of fear: fear of pain, fear of failure and fear of the unknown. Each of these fears can immobilize us, and an immobilized person can't make choices. When we are faced with such fears, we must find people to guide us in our struggles. We cannot expect them to face the fear for us, but we can ask them to support us as we face it.

Many people have difficulty taking hold because they don't know how. One way to find out is to get next to people who do. Watch them and ask them to teach you. Sometimes you may need professional help. Other times you may just need the teaching of a good friend. The important thing is to put yourself in a situation where you can acquire the needed know-how.

When Jim and Bonnie were having trouble in marriage, they realized they didn't know how to take hold of this new way of life. They began to look around their church for a couple whose relationship seemed to be the type they both wanted. It was scary, but they took the risk of asking another couple if they could spend time with them. The other couple was both willing and flattered. Both families gained from the experience.

If we have skills others could use, we should take the risk of offering them. It sounds pushy, doesn't it? But it doesn't have to be that way. What is pushy about offering to share your study skills with a person who says she doesn't know how to study, or sharing a parenting tip with a young father who doesn't know what to do with his two-year-old? We don't have to have all the answers, just the willingness to share a part of ourselves. The process of getting helper and helpee together will raise the self-esteem of both.

Another difficulty in taking hold is developing persistence. I am much better at talking than doing. I am also much better at starting than finishing. Because I know this about myself, I sometimes put off taking hold until the timing is perfect. Of course the perfect time never comes. The only answer seems to be to start today, continue tomorrow, keep on keeping on and finish when you can. Some good habits develop slowly and fade away quickly when ignored. We can ask a friend to hold us accountable until our feeble new habits are strong enough to take care of themselves.

Taking hold, then, involves these three elements: overcoming fears, learning skills and persisting until we develop good habits. Choices which take us through this process are bound to strengthen our self-esteem.

What about failure? We may have taken hold, but then our hands slipped and we let go. The key is not to let slips add up. Paul Hauck writes:

One of my clients had been trying to discipline himself to jog once a day. He kept this up for some months and felt very good about it. However, he was ill with the flu for a short time and could not jog for three days in a row. He saw this as no threat to his habit, so he was immediately back on the streets on the fourth day. But then the attractiveness of not doing it got to him because he remembered how nice it was not to jog on a cold winter night. Therefore one night he was not exactly up to it, and when the weather was a bit uncomfortable, he decided to let it go for that one night, promising himself to make up for it. And this he did. But several weeks after that he found himself again making excuses and he again skipped jogging. This continued intermittently until, in a matter of several months, he was down to jogging only once or twice a week and faltering seriously on his whole athletic program.[3] This story provides insight into why we give up on a good thing. The jogger did not quit just because he missed a day. He ultimately quit because he began to think about how good it felt not to have to put himself out to jog. He began to make excuses for not jogging, without admitting to himself that he was unwilling to pay the price to feel good physically. The more he allowed himself to listen to his excuses, the more he became the victim of his thoughts. When I miss a day of writing, the most helpful thing I can do is to say to myself, "I chose not to write." I don't have to excuse myself or punch myself; I simply need to decide whether I want to reach my writing goals. If I am not willing to give up, then I must be willing to get up. No excuses allowed.

Trusting the Sun

Finding my identity and developing self-esteem has to be more than thinking happy thoughts. As much as I believe in the power of positive thinking, I still maintain that we must believe not only in ourselves but also in the God who created us. Choosing who we want to be requires faith. Paul wrote, "I can do everything *through him who gives me strength*" (Phil 4:13).

Paul believed in himself, but he also believed in God as his source of strength. Faith is trusting God to help us become not only what we want to be but also all he has made us to be. It is an exciting adventure.

Applying faith to choice is, nonetheless, not easy. It goes against our basic human nature. Part of our survival instinct is to want to have all the answers before making a decision. In general, this is a good stance. God never intended us to be irrational or impulsive. In reality, however, we must make many choices with no way of predicting the outcome. This is often the case when we choose who we want to become. Faith says, "This seems like the direction God is giving me; I want to step forward. I may not make it, but even if I don't, God will still be with me." Faith also says, "I'm going to try. I owe it to God, and I owe it to myself."

Starting into the woods on a hike in the predawn darkness can be frightening. It seems so forbidding, and the trail is distinct only for a short distance. Can I really trust the morning rays of the sun to arrive by the time I reach the ravine? They were there yesterday, but what if they don't show up today? Trusting God is like trusting the sun. God has always been faithful, and yet I am still sometimes afraid of the dark. This is particularly true when I am in the dark of not really knowing or trusting myself. Is God as faithful as his creation, the sun? Since my teen years I have relied on Hebrews 13:8: "Jesus Christ is the same yesterday and today and forever." Having faith that God is a constant in life can help us make choices that will strengthen our hold on ourselves.

I believe that, within limits, we can choose who we want to be. Choice is one of the greatest privileges we have. When choice is exercised in our feelings, our thoughts and our behaviors, we can become the kind of stable people we want to be.

6
Becoming the Sum of My Commitments

———

PEOPLE WHO LACK self-acceptance often have trouble making commitments. When we are unsure who we are, it is hard to commit ourselves to anyone or anything. The reverse is also true: without commitment, it is hard to know who we are. When we are uncommitted, we are always waiting for life to happen instead of making it happen. We are out of control.

One summer my wife and I hiked out to an isolated lake in central British Columbia. A friend gave us a map, directions, fishing poles, a can of gasoline and a small outboard motor. "You will find the boat hidden in some weeds," he assured us. "It isn't in very good shape, but it will serve you fine." We were excited as we found the boat and carried it to the water's edge. We mounted and fueled the motor and were soon ready to explore the lake. We were thrilled to be in a part of God's creation where we could neither see nor hear another human being.

Sandy and I are not skilled at boating, so it took us awhile to realize something was wrong. I didn't seem to be able to control the boat. We were zigzagging or going in circles instead of going where we wanted to go. Pulling up the motor and reaching under the boat, I discovered the problem: the rudder had fallen off. At this point I could do nothing but try to return to shore. But hard as I tried to control its direction, the boat still drifted and circled. The more frustrated I became, the more I oversteered and the less control I had. It was a long trip back to the water's edge.

The only other time I felt that frustrated and out of control was when I wasn't committed to anything. I felt like the driver of a rudderless boat. In this chapter we will look at the way commitment or lack of commitment affects identity and self-acceptance. We will then offer guidelines for evaluating our commitments and developing priorities that contribute to self-acceptance.

Anyone Can Stay in Bed

When we are not committed to anything, it is hard to know when we are missed. We begin to feel invisible. Men who lose a job they have been committed to for years often suffer from a real lack of attachment. With no place to go, their self-esteem wavers and they begin to feel down on themselves.

As my father grew older, he decided to take a walk each day. At first he did this to help himself physically. However, he soon discovered a group of people who gather each morning at the restaurant on the corner. Now he walks there to share a cup of coffee and listen to their concerns. He doesn't give them advice; he just listens and cares. He is committed to these people. They need him, and they miss him when he doesn't show up. His commitment has given him purpose and a sense of worth.

Without commitment self-worth suffers because uncommitted people are not sure that they have something to offer. Depressed people often say they don't want to be bothered with commitments, but at the same time they can't find anything better to do than stay in bed. Anyone can stay in bed. When you are committed to something or someone, you want to get out of bed. This desire is fueled by the feelings of accomplishment you have after fulfilling your commitment. I often say to Sandy, "I didn't feel like getting up this morning, but once I was at my meeting I really felt like staying up." I am invigorated by using the gifts God has given me.

When Jim was asked to join a small-group Bible study, he was reluctant and frightened. It would have been easier to say no, but somehow he couldn't. "Oh well," he thought, "it is only for six weeks, and I can stand anything that long." Initially he thought of himself only as an observer. That was comfortable, but it didn't increase his feelings of worth. Anyone can watch.

As he got involved in the group, however, the leader began to pull him into the discussions. Jim found that he could read the passage being studied and answer questions in a way that the group understood. He began to realize he had some good insights that needed to be shared. By the end of the six weeks, he felt as if he was just started. Without that initial commitment, tentative though it was, he might never have learned he had something to offer.

Jim's situation shows why commitment is so important to self-acceptance. Without commitment, we lose opportunities to grow. At one time or another most of us have been reluctant to get involved in a project or relationship. But once involved we found we grew in an important area. Commitment usually results in growth, just as exercise produces muscle.

As the result of his commitment to the study group, Jim grew spiritually. He learned more about God and himself. He also grew in his relationship with the other group members.

I know you can be overcommitted. It is possible to say yes to more things than you can handle. I have discovered, however, that I sometimes say yes to familiar things and no to the unknown. If I were to turn this around, my growth would probably be stimulated. Commitment and growth usually go hand in hand.

Commitment also results in expanded horizons. Where there is no commitment, the view is usually ingrown and narrow. One Sunday I heard a man at church say, "Before I got involved with this church, I never realized how exciting life could be." He has become a visionary. He had all kinds of ideas on how to help people, new classes to start and projects to undertake. The problem now is keeping him from spreading himself too thin.

How is the view from the front porch of your mind? Can you see possibilities out there? If not, it may be because you have not committed yourself to anything.

Depressed people have narrow horizons. Depressed people usually break their commitments, even to things they like to do. When a friend called to break a date to play handball for no apparent reason, I knew he was in trouble. I challenged him to play even if he was depressed. By the time we had finished playing, the enjoyment had lifted his spirits enough that he was ready to take on his next commitment for the day. The domino theory works: each fulfilled commitment gives energy to move to the next one.

Fear of Failure
Commitment also affects our self-esteem by enabling us to overcome our fear of failure. One of the most healthy phrases a person can utter is, "I'll try." Trying requires commitment, and commitment helps us attack the fears that often immobilize us. Betty resisted any commitment to her sorority because she feared she couldn't do a good enough job. This fear was stronger than her desire for recognition. Finally a sorority sister said, "Betty, you need to do it—for us and for you." She succumbed to the pressure, said yes, and then began to realize that she could handle the situation quite easily. Without the commitment, she might never have overcome her fears. It was still hard for her to

say yes to the next opportunity, but with each new commitment and resulting success her fears weakened and she grew in self-acceptance. Fear of failure is an enemy to self-esteem, but it can be attacked by commitment.

Most of us have been frightened at the prospect of being in a new activity—even one we really wanted to do. Someone has said, "If you never experience fear, you don't understand life." However, there is a difference between experiencing fear and being controlled by fear. When we are controlled by fear, our self-esteem plummets. If we commit ourselves and challenge the fear, our self-esteem rises.

I don't like fear, but neither do I like the empty feeling I sometimes have when I have no commitment. I am willing to put up with the fear, if necessary, in order to accomplish my goals.

The biggest problem a lack of commitment can cause is to keep us from fulfilling our divine purpose. Divine purpose? Look at what Jesus said about his purpose for us: "I have come that they may have life, and have it to the full" (Jn 10:10).

God wants to improve the quality of our lives. He wants to give us spiritual and psychological abundance, not poverty. He has saved us, and he calls us to serve him: "[God] . . . has saved us and called us to a holy life" (2 Tim 1:9). This is not because of how good we are, but because he has a purpose for us. Self-worth comes as we realize we can serve him by using the gifts he has given us. We may wish we had other gifts, but that is not the point. God asks us only to commit ourselves to using what we know we have.

Too many of us say, "I'll serve God when . . ." Will we really? Changing circumstances will not cause us to serve God. We must decide to serve him and commit ourselves to him now. When we commit ourselves, he will begin to unveil his purpose for us.

In *Spiritual Gifts and the Church,* Bridge and Phypers write:
Situations will arise in our service to Christ, in which we need to act in a particular role. As long as we are not inhibited by

nervousness, doubt, or unbelief, we may well expect that the appropriate response to the situation will become possible. . . .

Perhaps most of all the individual Christian needs to remember that the Holy Spirit is sovereign, free, unpredictable, mysterious. He "apportions to each one individually as he wills" (1 Cor 12:11). He raises up church officers to exercise certain roles, anoints individuals to meet particular situations, directs seemingly natural abilities into channels of loving service, powerfully demonstrates divine intervention in critical situations, and enables Christians to accomplish deeds otherwise impossible.[1]

Probably the greatest commitment you and I need to make if we want to see God's purpose fulfilled in us is to be available. God seems to work in my life when I hold still long enough for him to do so. Talking to him every day helps, and so does reading and studying the Bible. When I do that, I get a clearer awareness of what he has in store for me. It is not magical; it is just a process of assimilation. When I see God's purposes more clearly, and when I see myself as I will be when he equips me and gives me gifts, I'm eager to commit myself to specific tasks. My efforts to serve don't always turn out perfectly, but I usually have a sense that God knows what he is doing. When I know he knows what he is doing, I feel worthwhile for being on his team.

Evaluating Priorities
Part of being committed is setting priorities. This world contains people who are committed to some very strange things. Some people are committed to the status quo. Others are committed to change. Not every commitment will increase our sense of self-worth. How do we decide what to commit ourselves to?

We have already discussed the starting place—*finding God's purpose*. This is not necessarily easy. God's purpose for us may be many-faceted, and it is constantly being revealed. The key is to set priorities that are in line with that purpose.

One of God's purposes for me is to help people on a one-to-one basis. He also has used me to help groups of people through public speaking and writing. These three things add up to one thing: my purpose is to communicate. However, at times I have been asked to set priorities that would take me away from that important task. Others will control me and set my priorities if I do not make an active choice to take control of that area of my life. If I want to know who I am, I dare not let other priorities for me contradict who I believe I need to be.

I am often asked the question, "Do I dare follow my interests?" My answer is clear. *Follow your interests.* I don't think that you dare ignore them.

Our interests are a part of who we are. They grow out of our personalities and experiences. They are dynamic in that new experiences can cause dormant interests to spring to life.

When Marsha entered college, she wanted to become a teacher because she knew teachers had many opportunities to serve God. But the more she prepared for a career in education, the more she realized she wasn't really interested in teaching. She came to the university counseling center for help. Together we evaluated her interest patterns. She came out high in the artistic and domestic categories, which led her to investigate possibilities in interior decorating.

After deciding to become an interior designer she said, "You will never know how good it feels to be free to do something I really want to do. I've always wanted to work with rooms and furniture, but my parents sent me clear messages that God would bless me only in teaching." God showed Marsha that he will bless her with the interests she has. This has freed her to step out to see what an interior decorator can do for God. Her commitment is strong because she has her priorities firmly in mind.

What will it take to pursue a given opportunity? Will I ever know if I don't try to develop my gifts in that area? As I develop them, I am following another important guideline for evaluating priorities: *follow your gifts and see where they take you.*

Bob was a fairly good amateur photographer. When he entered the Navy he took a photography class, and his talents blossomed. He became a Navy photographer and later made a career in industrial photography. Look what he would have missed if he had said, "Oh, well, it's interesting but I probably don't have the ability."

Not all gifts that need developing have vocational potential. Consider the importance of developing the gift of hospitality or a capacity for forming relationships. As we see these gifts develop, they may become priorities. Norman Wakefield has underscored the need to develop our potential in the area of listening. He writes:

> One of my goals in writing this book is to get Christians excited about the potential of developing their listening ability. Many people pay high fees to seek the expertise of listening specialists; we call these specialists counselors, psychologists, or psychiatrists. I am enthusiastic about helping nonspecialists increase their listening skills, because I know the power of effective listening. I am certain it is a very significant form of ministry available to anyone who would like to develop it.[2]

As we develop skills in a given area, we will sometimes need to set short-range priorities until we can understand how a gift fits into the total picture. After making the necessary commitment, we will learn what options may be open to us.

For years I wanted to write a book. I had been told I had some skill, but I never committed myself to the "learn by doing" process. Once I made the commitment and began to write, I realized I needed to reorganize my entire priority system to make room for more writing. This may be short-term (I might run out of things to say) or it may be long-term. All I know is that the process of developing the interest and the gift is exciting. It is good for self-esteem, and I don't even mind the royalty checks.

Another way to evaluate is to *look for opportunities*. If music is a priority, we should look for opportunities to use our musical abilities. We may begin to see how they fit into God's purpose. If we have opportunity to sing—we should sing. If to direct, then direct. If we like to compose, then composing. If we find success in a given area, then we should try it some more. If it doesn't seem to fit, then we can look for new possibilities. The key is to look for opportunities and try them out.

Let me offer a word of caution: opportuity is not to be confused with being easy. Some opportunities are just plain hard work. A friend who seeks to become a concert pianist says, "Playing the piano is harder work than digging ditches." But when he gets a chance to play in public he says, "I have a great opportunity here." Some opportunities may come to you on a silver platter, but most are hidden underground. We have to dig for them. In any event, as we look for opportunities we will come to know ourselves better.

You Can't Do It All

A fifth guideline in evaluating priorities is to *try to align them with one another*. There are a thousand things I would like to do. The problem is that I can't do them all. Some things conflict with one another. To solve this problem I have to look at the broader picture and see how each opportunity might affect the others. The problem requires energy as well as scheduling. If I spend all my energies at my work, I may have no time for the family. If I invest heavily in furthering my education, I may not have time for developing my spiritual life.

Some commitments, though worthwhile, can be overdone. If a little exercise is good, is a lot of exercise better? Not necessarily—it depends how it fits into the total picture. John likes to play basketball with his friends. It helps release the tension from his demanding job. The more he played, the more he wanted to play, until suddenly he was confronted by his angry wife. Why should she have to stay home by herself every evening? The answer was clear: she shouldn't. John never intended to neglect her; he just hadn't aligned his priorities. Fortunately, they dealt with the problem before it was too late. Many couples don't.

I have found it helpful to limit the number of extra responsibilities I accept at one time. By "extra" I mean responsibilities beyond God, family, church, my profession and physical maintenance. I like to serve my community and Christian organizations, but I can't serve all the good causes at once. It is important to control my choices rather than letting them control me.

The following steps can help one evaluate his or her commitments: list them and write the cost of each in terms of time and energy. Also assign a value to each one on a one-to-ten scale to see the value gained in relation to the time and energy spent. Draw a line between related activities. Put a minus sign by activities that detract from each other and a plus sign by those that support each other. If an activity detracts from another activity which you highly value, you might consider giving up the activity of lesser value.

The purpose of all this is to know what we are doing. Overcommitted people often struggle with problems of self-acceptance, just like uncommitted people. Overcommitment can cause us to feel terrible because we know we can't do a good job at everything. Blessed is the person who has the right amount of commitments, for he or she shall remain committed.

One additional guideline has proven helpful: *be committed to a group of people.* People sharpen people. Lone rangers are usually dull. We all need the challenge and the encouragement that only a group can give. Staying committed is difficult without the support of those of a like mind.

How does commitment to a group affect self-esteem? Sandy said, "It helps me to know that a group of people who know me deeply also care deeply. It helps to know there are people who want me to be all I can be."

Bill was reluctant to make a commitment to a group at first, but when he finally did, he found them very helpful. They listened to him and at times challenged him to learn to listen more to them. At first this was threatening, but then he began to realize how much he needed what they had to offer. "A small group can keep you honest," he said. "I guess I needed that to grow, even though I wouldn't admit it to myself." A small group helps us focus priorities and keep heading toward them.

Commitment is essential. Through a look at commitments, we begin to grasp who we really are. In a very real way, we are the sum of our commitments.

7
Created to Grow

THE PERSONAL-GROWTH movement of the late sixties and seventies sent people plunging into self-discovery. Some liked what they found. Others were left in shambles.

The growth movement represented a challenge to Freudian psychology. If Freud was right, basic personality is set by age seven. Freud would think it was pretty silly for thousands of young and not-so-young adults to put time and money into finding themselves through T groups, nude marathons, sensitivity training and self-awareness encounters. What if, after all this effort, we found that Freud was right—personal growth past the age of seven is impossible? Or what if psychological determinism is correct, and not even children can freely choose to change? Are all our attempts to change doomed before they start?

The God of Growth

Many psychologists say no. Lazarus and Fay write:

> Human beings, unlike any other species on earth, have the unique capacity for instant change. People are capable of making immediate and long-lasting decisions that can have a profound influence on their emotional well-being. In other words, even if someone has responded incorrectly or "neurotically" to a given situation for many years on end, a systematic corrective exercise can often undo the problem there and then. We have seen this happen dozens of times.[1]

The Christian answer to these important questions is also an emphatic no. We believe in a personal God who is continually active in the lives of his children. The creator of the universe and the sustainer of all life does not allow his work to be confined by our early childhood experience. We are dynamic creations made for change. In fact it is the dynamic, changing aspect of our person that often causes us to question our identity. If I am not the exact same person I was yesterday, then who am I?

Change can make it difficult for me to accept myself. Marge was raised in a strong Christian home and was taught basic Christian beliefs from her early childhood. Along with sound, biblically based doctrine, she was also taught some Christian traditions as though they were Scripture. Marge sailed through college and nurses' training and soon found herself serving God in "full-time Christian service." The life of faith was easy until some of her Christian traditions began to fail her. She attended church, prayed ritualistically and read her Bible as though it were magic. Marge believed that if she followed God, all her dreams would come true. She also believed that what she did was more important than who she was. So she continued to smile and to work until some of her dreams began to fade. Where was the young man she was certain God would provide if she just kept doing God's work? Where was the sense of satisfaction in her work? Why was it becoming difficult to pray? Why was she depressed to the point of not being able to get up and get going in the morning? Marge's vocational goals began to waver. She questioned her abilities as a nurse. Her self-esteem also began to crumble as she started to wonder if she had anything to offer anyone.

What does all this have to do with growth? Marge's life was following a pattern I have often observed. She had gone from having all the answers to feeling that she didn't have any answers at all. She was now ready to grow.

As Marge and I talked she began to realize that God was with her even when things weren't going well. She also came to realize that he loved her for who she was as well as for what she did. As these beliefs took root, she began to enjoy her work more and was willing to take the risk of entering into a relationship with a man. Her goals didn't change, but she grew to the point of understanding that she was a valuable person regardless of whether or not her goals were met. Her foundation for life became what God was doing for her, not what she was doing for God. The negative experiences of instability and self-doubt proved to be the catalyst for growth. (See figure 2.)

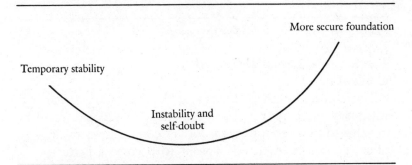

Figure 2: Growth through Negative Experience

Positive experience also affects growth. When Jim came to college he didn't understand his potential. Life had always been easy, so he had floated on his successes. College provided him with the first true test. It challenged him socially, academically and emotionally. When the challenges came he was successful, and he liked the experience. He wasn't floating now, however; he had to learn to swim. Jim constantly watched other successful people. Sometimes he asked them to help him learn. As a result his grades improved and he became well known and influential on campus. Life was exciting because he was challenged and because he accepted each challenge to grow.

This type of growth is in figure 3. Growth through positive experience is like walking up stairs. You may not know where the top is, but you know there is another step in front of you.

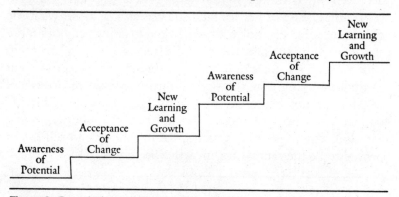

Figure 3: Growth through Positive Experience

Ten Steps to Personal Growth
1. Want it.

The phrase "you have to want it" has become popular with athletes who recognize it costs something to succeed. You have to want to grow too; growth doesn't come automatically. Sacrifice is often necessary. If I want to become a better public speaker, I may have to sacrifice parties and recreation to practice speech. I may have to pay for voice lessons or for someone to videotape me so I can learn about my nonverbal communication. Who knows, I may even need to take a course in logic. At any rate, I have to want it.

Many people want to grow in relationships. Those who succeed are the ones who do more than talk about their desire to grow. They want it enough that they get involved with people and take a healthy, critical look at their ways of relating and seek out options for change.

Wanting growth isn't everything, but it is the place to start. Evaluate your desire to grow. Do you want it enough to discipline yourself? Is sacrifice part of your vocabulary? You have to want it. Don't take my word for it; listen to Paul:

Do you not know that in a race all the runners run, but only one gets the prize? Run in such a way as to get the prize. Everyone who competes in the games goes into strict training. They do it to get a crown that will not last; but we do it to get a crown that will last forever. Therefore I do not run like a man running aimlessly; I do not fight like a man beating the air. No, I beat my body and make it my slave so that after I have preached to others, I myself will not be disqualified for the prize. (1 Cor 9:24-27)

2. Be vulnerable.

The most comfortable thing for me to do is not to grow at all. I'm used to being underdeveloped. I'm used to my inadequacies. I can even tolerate most of my failures. To grow means to become vulnerable. I may have to give up some weakness which serves a real purpose for me. For example, I may get more attention when I am weak than when I am strong. To be vulnerable means to let others know where my growth points are. It is easier to play the "I'm OK" game than to let others help me learn. We tend to give the picture either of having it all together or of having nothing together. The more productive picture is to see myself and allow others to see me as one who wants to grow. What does it take to become vulnerable enough to want to grow? Eugene Kennedy writes:

Taking risks is the key to entering life more deeply, experiencing it in a happier and fuller fashion. When we no longer hide the truth about ourselves, others can see us truly, perhaps for the first time. We hear that recognition in the things people say when they glimpse something of each other's true personality. "You're not like everybody else," friends and lovers say to each other. "You're different." This is the kind of affirmation that comes to us when we give ourselves a chance at life.[2]

3. *Know yourself.*

Have you ever talked to a friend about a third person? I'm not talking about gossip. I mean a productive conversation in which both of you share your admiration as well as your hopes for the other person. Maybe your conversation went something like this:

"Pete is really coming along, isn't he?"

"Boy, he sure is. He relates to people so much better than he used to. It's like he has broken out of his shell."

"He needs just a little more confidence, and he will have a strong influence on others."

If I overheard your conversation I would have two questions. Does Pete know he is coming along? Does Pete know he needs to keep growing in self-confidence? If he doesn't, he needs to. We don't usually grow unless we know we need to. Take a physical analogy. If Sue's golf game is off and she doesn't know why, it is pretty hard to improve. However, if she discovers that she needs to correct her back swing, she can then practice in a way that will promote growth and improvement.

We can also get to know ourselves by listening as we talk with others and by watching our actions and reactions. Are there skills we do not have that we would like to have? If so, we can set some goals.

Two cautions are needed in regard to getting to know ourselves. First, we must realize that we can spend entirely too much time in self-examination and too little time in living. Taking time to think seriously about who we are and how we would like to be is not a full-time job. It is easy to get stuck on the things we cannot change instead of looking for those things we can change. Such introspection is not productive. We need to think about the possibilities, not the problems.

There is a great difference between looking within to see possible areas for growth and stewing over things we can't change. Scripture asks this helpful question: "Who of you by worrying can add a single hour to his life?" (Mt 6:27).

The second caution is to avoid comparisons. I repeat this over and over again because making comparisons is a major spiritual and emotional problem. People who compare themselves with others all the time are not healthy. We need to grow for our own sakes and not so that we will be equal to or better than someone else.

4. Look for misconceptions.

Do I like being wrong? No more than you do. Most of us will do almost anything to avoid the appearance of being incorrect about anything. Unfortunately, we are often wrong about many things. Misconceptions create a major barrier to self-acceptance. If we want to grow, we need to understand the misconceptions stunting our growth. Victor Raimy writes, "Misconceptions about the self may drastically and unrealistically limit the kinds of behavior an individual is willing to engage in, or they may relentlessly force him into unwise behavior which leads to perpetual defeat."[3]

If I have the misconception that I must be an excellent conversationalist before I can open my mouth, I will never improve my conversational skills. If I challenge this misconception and replace it with the belief that I can learn to be a better conversationalist by engaging in conversations with many people, I am set to grow. The key is to tell myself the truth.

What misconceptions prevent us from growing? Lazarus and Fay list some common myths (misconceptions) which lead many people to doubt their capacity to change.

Myth #1: If you have knowledge and understanding—in other words, if you know why you are the way you are, or why you do the things you do, or why you feel the way you feel—then you will change.

Myth #2: If you don't know the reasons behind your behavior, you won't change.

Myth #3: It takes a long time to change. After all, you have had problems for a long time.

Myth #4: If you change fairly quickly, it is superficial and it won't last.

Myth #5: It is frequently impossible to change. "This is the way I am, and this is the way I'll always be."

Myth #6: If you are middle-aged or older, it is too late to change.[4]

These myths need to be replaced with the belief that God is interested in helping us become all we can be and that he wants our cooperation. Janice was almost immobilized by fear because she had the misconception that she would fail at anything she tried. She also believed that if she failed, her family would abandon her. I encouraged her to challenge these misconceptions by reminding herself that God would help her succeed and by admitting that neither he nor her family would leave her. This new correct view has enabled Janice to live a normal life and to grow to the point of feeling good about herself.

Melissa, my daughter, hung perilously on the face of the rock she was trying to climb. Only her fingertips, toes and the safety rope were preventing her from falling. "I can't make it," she cried. "Maybe so," I called to her, "but you have to try." She regrouped emotionally and reached for the next handhold. She pulled herself up and cleared the ledge. I hugged her as she looked up at me through tears of fear and joy. "I was wrong," she said; "I'm a better climber than I thought." She had corrected a basic misconception which said, "I can't." This experience cleared the way for her to try new challenges both physically and emotionally. She is growing because her new conception says, "I can."

5. Develop a plan.

Many would like change to occur with little or no involvement on their part. Chris said, "Why can't God just make it happen?" I asked him if he thought God ever asked, "Why doesn't Chris just make it happen?" It was a new thought to Chris.

Planning for growth or change is difficult because there are no perfect plans. Sometimes we have to begin by deciding to do *something,* even if we are not sure it is the right thing. There are no assurances that the plan will work. As we begin to carry out our plan, however, we will see new possibilities. God can direct us best when we are moving. As with power steering, it is hard to turn the wheel without the engine running. Once the engine is running, steering is easy.

Ted wants to learn to communicate better. He decides to start with Bill. Ted knows that both of them have time after class so he asks Bill to have a Coke. Bill says no, but Ted asks him about the next day. When Bill asks what he wants to talk about, Ted says he just wants to get better acquainted. Who knows—Bill may want the same thing.

Once the time and place are set, then Ted can plan a strategy. What topics could he talk about? What questions could he ask? He wants to draw Bill out since it has to be his conversation as well as Ted's.

What else can Ted do? He reads a book on communication to get some new ideas. He picks one or two things he hadn't thought about before, and tries them out when with Bill.

The last part of Ted's plan is to ask Bill if he would like to get together again. If so, Ted can continue to learn from this relationship. Bill will learn too. Both of them probably need to hear and be heard.

A plan for growth can be quite simple, but if there is no plan, there may be no growth.

6. Take risks.

Can you imagine a baseball player who wasn't willing to take the risk of striking out? A mountain climber who wouldn't risk falling? An author who wouldn't risk criticism? A student who wouldn't risk a bad grade on a test? What about a friend who wouldn't risk rejection? Life is risky, and we must be willing to take risks if we expect to progress.

Many well-formulated plans for growth never succeed because

the planner cannot or will not take the risks involved to set the plan in action.

Mark has planned for months to talk to his father about some unresolved issues between them. He feels this conversation is essential if he is to grow emotionally. "I just have too many strong feelings about things that happened with Dad," Mark said. "They are like a cancer that has to be removed." If Mark feels so strongly about his cancer, then why hasn't he done something about it? Because Mark is so afraid of losing his father that he can't take the risk of talking with him and healing their relationship.

Usually when you take a deep breath and do the feared thing, you find that it wasn't as bad as you thought. Most risks turn out OK if you follow a well-thought-out plan based on God's input received through prayer and Scripture. When I ask myself, "What is the worst thing that could happen?" I usually conclude that the worst thing would be not to take the risk and thus not to grow.

I use friends to help me evaluate risks. Their input is often valuable because they can stand back from the situation and see it more clearly than I can. I also learn from my friends that different people see different things as risky. Some worry about outcomes. Some worry about what people think. Others seem not to worry about anything at all. The key is to balance the feared risks with the realities of the situation. What are the risks of doing nothing? Can I expect support from God? Can I expect help from my friends? Even if the risks are great right now, what is the long-range outlook? Sometimes it all boils down to this: it is better to take the risks than to risk not growing.

As we begin to take risks, we should carefully evaluate what happens. Afterward we can determine which risks were real and which imagined. How many fears were based on reality? Real dangers can be faced with prayer, recognizing that God will protect. "The LORD is my strength and my shield; my heart trusts in him, and I am helped. My heart leaps for joy and I will give thanks to him in song. The LORD is the strength of his people, a fortress of salvation for his anointed one" (Ps 28:7-8). Anxieties (unfounded fears) need to be turned back to God. "Cast all your anxiety on him because he cares for you" (1 Pet 5:7). Casting our anxieties on God means choosing not to focus upon our fears but rather on the fact that God can help us handle even the most frightening possibility. Taking risks requires taking control of our thoughts and feelings by focusing on positive possibilities rather than on potential problems.

7. Evaluate your efforts.

The process of growth is like checking out my archery skills. After I have made an attempt, I need to look at the target to see how close I came. I often ask my children, "Were you able to accomplish what you set out to do?" I want them to evaluate their efforts. If the answer is yes, I want them to rejoice in their success. If the answer is no, I want them to figure out why they were not successful. In bowling, have you ever closed your eyes after trying to make a 7-10 split? Unless you open them again, you will never know how close you came. Even if you are successful, you will not know why unless you are willing to examine the results of your ball. We lose many opportunities for growth when we aren't willing to evaluate our efforts.

Paul Hauck writes, "You never fail as long as you are trying. Each trial teaches you something if you study your behavior. You're getting valuable feedback from each effort, and this information is a small segment of success. Don't knock it. If you repeat the trials often enough, you add up little successes on top of little successes until they become noticeable. The upshot is that you are failing only when you are not trying, never otherwise."[5] Growth usually happens when we weave trying and evaluation together so that our next efforts can be even more on target.

Most evaluations are based on three simple questions: Did I hit the target? Do I know what worked and what didn't work? What changes might I make in order to be more successful? This evaluation process leads directly to our next step.

8. Recognize small gains.

Rarely is any attempt at growth totally successful or totally unsuccessful. There will be areas of success and areas of failure or lack of progress. The key is to recognize the gains, even if they are small, so we can build on them. If we do not recognize that our conversation skills are improving, we may not continue our efforts. Many people give up just short of success because they don't realize that large gains are made out of small ones. We should acknowledge even a thread of growth, because such threads are woven into the cloth of success.

Recognizing small gains is also useful because it causes us to rehearse the steps we have taken. Each rehearsal strengthens our behavior pattern and sets the stage for further growth. Even if we don't know what we did that worked, we should keep doing it and we will probably figure it out. Growth can be mysterious at times, but most of the mystery can be solved by studying the gains that have been made.

9. Start over when necessary.

Every person needs to experience at least one total flop. It is good for the soul. Once I have fallen flat on my face, I am likely to be more humble, and I may also learn not to take myself so seriously. Many things in life are more traumatic than failure, and yet we feel if we fail there is no tomorrow. In discussing fear of failure, Charles Swindoll writes, "Great accomplishments are often attempted but only occasionally reached. What is interesting (and encouraging) is that those who reach them are usually those who missed many times before. Failures, you see, are only temporary tests to prepare us for permanent triumphs."[6]

We learn unhealthy attitudes toward failure because parents and teachers try to motivate us through fear of failure. "Johnny, if you don't do your homework, you will fail, and then what will you do?" It is too bad Johnny can't say, "I'll start over. Failing doesn't mean I am a failure." But whether or not we see failure as the end of the world, it is still a problem with which we must contend. Our response to failure in our attempts to grow will largely determine how successful we will be. Starting over is the key.

I have learned a lot from watching my older son learn rock climbing. It takes great courage to face a vertical cliff, even with a safety rope. One thing I noticed was that he didn't start by saying, "I can't do it." He said, "I'll give it a try." At first he managed only a few feet before his fingertips and toes gave way. As he stood on the ground looking up, he said, "I'll bet I can get higher than that if I use a different handhold." His teacher encouraged him. This time he went even higher than he expected. He had to start over several times, but he did eventually succeed. He did not take his failures seriously. He saw them as learning experiences. Each time he started over, it was with new hope. When failure is confronted with that attitude, it usually leads to success.

One important guideline in starting over is to always take the time to ask if there are adjustments we need to make. Even though failure should not cause us to lose our self-esteem, hardly anyone can handle the effects of repeated failure in the same activity. We should start over, but start over thoughtfully.

10. Consolidate your gains.

At a conference designed to help couples grow in their marriages, a man asked this question: "Do I have to be working on something all the time? This growth business wears me out." His question was an eye opener. Is it OK to spend time just enjoying what you have accomplished?

I believe Scripture encourages us to sit back and appreciate the gains we have made. God said, "Work six days and then take a day of rest." He made us, so he must know we need that rest. I have found that nothing encourages me more than taking the time to celebrate my successes. As I savor the changes I have made, I am energized to move toward the changes I need to make.

A sense of progress is essential to feelings of self-worth. Sometimes I have to back away from the struggles before this sense of progress can develop. It is like trying to see growth in my children. I can usually see it best when I have been away from them for a while.

If we do not deliberately take the time to rest and enjoy our gains, we will probably become nonproductive. We may begin to avoid the work we are trying to do. We can only push ourselves so far. People who try to push, push, push end up responding to their fatigue, but they are not resting or enjoying their accomplishments. In fact, they usually feel guilty because their fatigue is preventing them from accomplishing anything. It is much better to plan our rest and then to enjoy it.

Not only is growth possible; it is God's way. We have been created for change. Our old selves may not be that bad, but by following the steps I have suggested we will become all we can be. As this happens, we will know who we are, and we will like who we see in the mirror.

8
Identity and Self-Worth in a High-Tech Society

IN HIS HELPFUL BOOK *Making Vocational Choices,* Dr. John L. Holland writes, "The goal of vocational guidance—matching men and jobs—remains the same despite much talk, research, and speculation. Our devices, techniques, classifications, and theories are more comprehensive and sophisticated than in the days of Parsons (1909), the founder of vocational guidance, but the goal is still one of helping people find jobs that they can do well and that are fulfilling."[1]

As I read Dr. Holland's statement, two phrases in the last sentence caught my eye. The goal is to help people "find jobs that they can do well" and find jobs "that are fulfilling." Both conditions have tremendous implications for personal identity and self-worth. People who are not working at fulfilling jobs don't usually feel good about themselves. People who do not experience a sense of mastery in their jobs struggle with low self-esteem.

Our society has trained us to place tremendous importance on having a good job and doing it well. We are a society of doers—sometimes to a fault. We tend to derive our self-worth from what we do rather than who we are. But when this condition exists, we are in trouble, because technology tends to distract us from feelings of self-worth. Udo Middelmann has put things in proper perspective. He writes:

> When the Bible gives me a place and says who I am and affirms my identity not from the immediate surroundings but rather from God himself, then I come to what is so intimately linked with my identity—the need to be creative over God's universe. And this is work. Just as God expressed himself and his character in his creation and in his revelation to man, so the image of God in man must be expressed, must be externalized. It is not a threat to me if I work, if my identity is no longer tied to the job that I do, the part in society that I play or the body in nature that I am. In fact, all of a sudden, work and creativity, so intimately linked together, become a challenge.[2]

From this vantage point we can examine some challenges to identity and self-worth posed by our high-tech society. We will then look at some alternative responses to our current situation which may help us respond to the challenge and be the people God made us to be.

The Challenge of Unemployment
Our era is characterized not only by the emergence of the computer but also by an unstable economy plagued by high levels of inflation, interest and unemployment. For hundreds of thousands of people, the number-one challenge is to find a job. Unemployment and low self-esteem often go hand in hand. It is hard to feel good about myself in a work-oriented society when I don't have a job.

Three groups of people have been particularly hurt in the current unemployment crunch. First are the young. Entry-level occupations are scarce, and both high-school and college graduates are having trouble finding jobs that pay above minimum wage. The effect on self-esteem is obvious. One young friend said, "I had looked forward to beginning my life after college, but without a job I'm right back where I've always been—dependent on my parents." The prolonged adolescence resulting from the unemployment problem has led many young people to prolonged struggles with self-worth. Our society is not used to delaying gratification, and nothing demands the ability to delay gratification more than the inability to find a job. Marcie said, "All those things I have bought for my first apartment are just going to have to stay packed up."

Middle- and upper-management people have also been hit hard by unemployment. These are the people who were previously noted for their success, the upwardly mobile. The crisis in white-collar unemployment has created a new social phenomenon, the misplaced achiever. One former company president said, "I was OK when the board of directors voted to close the company, but what I wasn't ready for was the total rejection I felt after pounding the pavement for months and not even coming up with a lead. The pressure on me and my family has been almost unbearable."

The third group hit hard by unemployment is factory workers. This category contains many ethnic minorities and therefore has a great impact upon the balance of wealth in our society. This group has had two enemies to battle: inflation, which leads to reduced demand for goods; and automation, which results in workers' being replaced by robots and other machines. Neither development is good for self-esteem. It is hard to face the fact that people don't want to buy what you are making. It is also hard to accept the fact that machines can do it faster and better.

All of the previously employed suffer another blow to self-esteem—the inability to afford many things they previously purchased and relied upon for feelings of self-worth. The unemployed may have to do without a new car, a video recorder or stylish clothes. In addition, their self-esteem is devastated even more by the threat of bill collectors and repossession. One person said, "For the first time in my life I was unable to get credit to buy what I wanted. I felt helpless and ashamed. I couldn't believe it was happening to me."

Lack of opportunity to produce and lack of financial power are realities which must be faced and overcome by nearly a tenth of all Americans at any given time. The challenge of unemployment has affected our society to such an extent that we have had to take another look at our belief that identity and self-worth are based on what we do. If we are only as valuable as what we do, we may be in deep trouble today. Undoubtedly we must build new foundations for our self-esteem.

Lack of Job Satisfaction

Lack of job satisfaction is another heavy challenge to self-esteem. Although this problem is not new, it is nevertheless very real in our current society. Let us look at three sources of job satisfaction: opportunity to see the completed product, opportunity to interact with other workers and opportunity to build a better mousetrap.

High-technology manufacturing demands that workers perform one task over and over again, usually at a high speed. This means that workers rarely have the opportunity to see the value of their work to the finished product. I asked one young man about his job. He said, "I stamp out computer chips." When I asked him what they were for, he didn't have the slightest idea. He was bored with his job and had no sense of satisfaction because he didn't see how important those computer chips really are.

Craftsmen have been replaced with machine operators. Although this may be necessary for economic survival in a highly competitive market, it is certainly not in the best interest of the worker's emotional health. When a job does not allow workers to see the total product, they will feel dissatisfied, bored, purposeless and, finally, worthless. If you work in such a job, you will have to find ways of viewing your work that will increase your sense of the value of what you do. I suggested that the young man who ran the computer-chip machine follow one of those chips to its destination. When he did so, he learned that his chip ended up in a hospital as part of the system used to monitor patients with heart problems. His job took on new meaning as he realized that his product was important and that it was being used for the sake of real people.

Opportunity to interact with other workers is a second source of job satisfaction affected by high-technology jobs. Jeff was disappointed when they remodeled the factory he worked in. He was even more disappointed to learn that half of his coworkers were being laid off. The new work environment was pleasant, and the machines were truly amazing once he learned how to run them. But gregarious Jeff, who had always talked fast and worked fast, now found himself shut up in a room full of dials, buttons and levers. The longer he stayed in this isolated setting, the more depressed he became. He said, "I just can't feel good about what I'm doing when I don't have anyone to share it with."

Jeff decided to keep the job because he had a young family to support, so I encouraged him to look for new ways to maintain friendships at work. He found that by coming to work a half hour early and by changing his break times he could keep up with his pals. This gave him the boost he needed to regain his feelings of value on the job. If you find yourself in a situation like Jeff's, use your creativity to try to restructure the work situation to meet your needs. Don't waste psychological energy bemoaning your fate or cussing the machines. Machines are a part of our future; we need to live with them without letting them control our feelings of self-worth. Instead, create new options for yourself. You will certainly increase your present job satisfaction. You may even create yourself a better job.

When our younger son, Mike, was ten, his mother and I saw him carry a number of unusual items to his room—boards, washers, fishing line, nails, screws, clothespins and a variety of tools. It was not unusual to see his creativity in action, but this time we had no idea what he was making. He closed his door and told us we couldn't come in until he finished his invention. We sipped another cup of coffee and tried to be patient. Finally the door swung open, and Mike stood there with a big smile on his face. "It works," he said. "Do you want to see it?" We eagerly went into his room. He stepped to the head of his bed, took hold of the ends of the fishing line, and magically pulled his covers into place.

"How do you like it?" he asked proudly.

"It's neat," we replied. "What do you call it?"

"It's an automatic bed maker," he said. "I've always hated to make my bed, and now I can do it just by pulling two strings."

God made us all with a desire to "build a better mousetrap." Genesis 1:28 records the fact that God told Adam and Eve to rule over his creation. "God blessed them and said to them, 'Be fruitful and increase in number; fill the earth and subdue it. Rule over the fish of the sea and the birds of the air and over every living creature that moves on the ground.'" Undoubtedly part of faithfully carrying out this responsibility is to find a better way of doing things.

What do you do if your job doesn't allow for creativity? Margaret was faced with this predicament. She had so much to do that it seemed she couldn't take time to figure out how to do it better. She was beginning to hate her work, and her self-esteem was bouncing off the bottom of the barrel. I knew her well enough to challenge her bluntly. "Make a choice," I said. "You can spend the rest of your life telling everyone how overworked and dissatisfied you are, or you can make some changes. Even if it costs you your job, you won't lose much."

She had a vacation day coming, so she drove to the beach and re-evaluated the whole situation. "I think better," she said, "with the ocean trickling over my toes." She came back with a new plan and a strategy for talking to her boss. Much to her surprise, her supervisor said, "I've been wondering what we could do. Let's try it!"

By taking the risk of trying to improve her situation, Margaret increased her job satisfaction greatly and also began to get a better hold on her own identity. "I can be more than just a paper shuffler," she said. "It's nice to know God gave me a brain." Middelmann stresses the importance of taking definite, even if small, creative steps:

Do you have trouble in the area of work and identity? Then begin with little things, little things you can manage, little things you can see. Become a worker in the street department and prune bushes along the street as one student did who came to live near us. In the evening, he came back and said, "Without my creativity in clipping bushes, that street would still have bushes hanging over the edge." You might say that's not very beautiful and not very stimulating, but to the person who has a profound question about whether he has any importance at all in modern society, it matters. One doesn't have to clip bushes all the rest of his life, but he begins with little things.[3]

All three sources of job satisfaction we have discussed are affected by the tremendous changes taking place in the world of work. The challenge to the modern worker's self-esteem is to maintain a sense of who he or she is and the value of what he or she does despite the absence of traditional reinforcers. Now more than ever Philippians 4:11-12 challenges us: "I am not saying this because I am in need, for I have learned to be content whatever the circumstances. I know what it is to be in need, and I know what it is to have plenty. I have learned the secret of being content in any and every situation, whether well fed or hungry, whether living in plenty or in want."

Where previously we might have been able to change jobs if we were not satisfied, today we may have to learn to enjoy the job we have or face having no job at all. Fortunately, it is possible to be content even with a job that does not provide intrinsic satisfaction. In such cases it is vital to believe the words which follow the verses cited above: "I can do everything through him who gives me strength" (Phil 4:13).

Need for Retraining

Most young Americans grow up with one of two ideas about life after high school. Some believe they will find a job and stay at that job as long as they want to. Others believe they will go to college or technical school and then go to work in their chosen profession or trade for as long as they want to. Both ideas are myths.

Job permanency is as illusive as job satisfaction. Many jobs disappear between the time a person begins school or training and the time he or she is ready to go to work. A West Coast newspaper headline revealed that ninety per cent of students in alternative high-school programs were being trained for jobs that would not exist in sufficient numbers by the time training was completed and would not exist at all in ten years. The need for retraining is fast becoming a way of vocational life at all levels from college professor to factory worker.

Retraining may be a blessing as well as a curse. New positions being created may be more exciting and offer more opportunities for personal fulfillment than outdated jobs, or they may be boring and repetitive. Take television or computer repair, for example. Industry has found that with solid-state electronic technology it is cheaper to replace the entire system, now contained in a slip-in electronic board, than to find the malfunction and repair it. What used to be a problem-solving job is now as simple as replacing a light bulb. Designers of such sophisticated systems no doubt have limitless opportunities for personal fulfillment, but the people who repair the systems no longer have a place to use their problem-solving skills.

In the past retraining usually meant a step upward with new

responsibilities and opportunities. Today this may no longer be the case. Whether one is stepping up, down or sideways, however, any change has implications for self-esteem and must be taken seriously. What are the implications of vocational retraining for self-esteem?

First, although change may be temporarily exciting, it may not be advantageous over the long run. Jane was excited when the director of nursing asked her to consider being retrained to perform a specific diagnostic test related to heart disease. Her excitement grew as she realized that the new test would save patients pain and decrease the possibility of death. Jane's pioneering spirit was also moved by thoughts of operating one of the first units of this type in her city. But Jane was cautious as well as excited. She arranged to observe the process for a day or two at a hospital in a neighboring city before making her decision. The observation helped her think through most of the pluses and minuses and come to a decision. The pluses were obvious: she wanted to learn something new that would directly benefit people, and she was flattered that she was chosen. When she curtailed her excitement, however, the minuses began to loom larger. In the new position she would have less patient and family contact. She would be performing a routine task and would therefore have less opportunity for creativity and problem solving. Her management skills would go unused because even if the new procedure took hold, there would be only one other person to supervise. Much to the dismay of the hospital, she turned down the opportunity.

I didn't have to tell Jane she had made a good decision. She knew her decision was right. The new job would not have satisfied the three most important components of her satisfaction with nursing: patient contact, opportunity to solve problems and staff management. Loss of any of these three elements would have affected her feelings of worth. Jane would have given up too much for a temporary reprieve from the pressures of her current position.

In our present economy retraining may be linked with a step down. Some companies attempt to keep employees even though their original jobs are no longer needed. While the employees are grateful to have steady work rather than to face unemployment, it is obvious that their self-esteem will suffer. It is hard to see ourselves as valuable persons when what we did or would like to do is no longer necessary.

Another blow to self-esteem occurs if people discover their academic background is inadequate to prepare them for the better retraining opportunities. A flood of fear may threaten to wash away what self-esteem is left. One friend said, "I was scared to death of college when I was eighteen. How do you think it feels to be forty-five and back on campus?" It would be an understatement to say that the need to retrain left him in crisis. If he survives, he will be the stronger for it. If he doesn't, only God knows how severe the blow to his self-worth will be. If you know someone in this type of situation, do not hesitate to give him or her lots of support.

We have discussed three main challenges to self-esteem posed by our high-tech society: unemployment, lack of job satisfaction and need for retraining. We can now look at some responses which may enable us not only to survive but even to thrive.

New Predicament, New Responses

I have been repeatedly challenged by individuals who choose to live above the circumstances rather than to succumb to the perils of daily life. I recently saw a bumper sticker that said, "If the world serves you lemons, then make lemonade." I like that survivor spirit. It encourages me to look for new responses to our current vocational predicament.

Develop avocational interests. If the challenges of our high-tech society prevent us from finding self-worth in our jobs, then we'd better turn elsewhere for satisfaction. One person said, "If my job is cut to six hours a day or four days a week, I will have that much more time to devote to hobbies or my family." Another person said, "There are so many things I have wanted to learn, and now I have the opportunity to learn them."

Adaptability is the key to solving this problem. When we face change at work, we need to change with it. We can do things the way we have always done them, or we can adapt to our situation. When my father was a young man, he had little time to pursue interests beyond his work. He could hardly find time for a game of baseball. Others with this pattern will need to carefully choose how to use their free hours. If they do not invest them, they will feel even more worthless, but if they look for new interests, they will find new satisfactions.

The disadvantages of a shortened work day or a part-time job can be overcome by creatively following other interests which might not otherwise be satisfied. I am impressed with the number of college students and new graduates who are using their free time to become involved in some form of Christian ministry. What would you like to do that you have been telling yourself you don't have time to do? Instead of talking about it, do it. You will be amazed how it will help your feelings of self-worth.

Volunteer for human service. Earlier I mentioned that the sixties was the period of commitment to causes. But by the latter half of the seventies it seemed no one would volunteer for anything. Making money once again became the in thing; older people were no longer visited, and children were left untutored. This public apathy, coupled with decreased budgets for human services, has created a crisis to which the church must respond. Where have the so-called good Samaritans gone? We must be concerned with others because Jesus asked us to be and because he promised to bless us if we are: "If anyone gives a cup of cold water to one of these little ones because he is my disciple, I tell you the truth, he will certainly not lose his reward" (Mt 10:42).

One blessing that comes from loving others as ourselves is a restoration of self-worth. Modern technology gives us the opportunity to engage in this creative alternative, if we are willing to get involved once again. Janet, a hospital nurse, tutors black children in North Portland. Is it worth it? "Yes," she says, "some days my job gets pretty routine. Watching monitors isn't always exciting, and dealing with death can be stressful. But when I am with those children, I feel life. I know I am making a difference for them, and consequently they are making a difference for me."

Consider opportunities abroad. It is no secret that most of the world's wealth is in the hands of a small percentage of the population. In fact, only the wealthy can develop a high-tech society—the rest of the world is too busy trying to get enough food to stay alive. If you are tired of your rat race, why not help others in their race for survival? Why not use your skills to make a difference in the lives of some people in Third World countries? It can be a wonderful way to receive a new perspective on life.

You can make a difference, you know. Not for the whole world, but for an important few. If you do not find satisfaction in pushing buttons, why not help people? If you are tired of programming a computer, why not teach others how to do it? Each year thousands of people volunteer to go as short-term missionaries. They leave their jobs or take time off to be support persons for established missionaries or to serve national Christians. They come back with an entirely different view of life, a new identity and a new sense of their worth. They are now world Christians. And guess what—they are not bored.

These are only a few possible responses to the challenges of our modern technological society. The most important thing is to respond. Too many people sit around waiting for something good to happen to them. They want things to change, but they are unwilling to take the necessary risks to help create the change they desire. Don't be like them—do something.

The skeptic says, "These are fine ideas, but they don't fit my situation. I have a dead-end job, and there is nothing I can do about it. I am a victim of the system." I think skeptics are copping out. After they try five new ideas, they can tell me it is impossible to find satisfaction.

Good things don't come easy, and every time we give up, self-esteem drops a notch. We can't allow ourselves to moan about conditions and backbite people without seeking change. Rather than allowing the system to seduce us into negative thought-patterns which will destroy our self-esteem and our sense of who God made us to be, let us be creative enough to take charge of our lives.

It is fine to push buttons or watch machines, but if a strong sense within us says, "I am more than a button pusher," then we should act on that. We can push the buttons if necessary to put bread on the table, but we can involve ourselves at other levels too. Reading, writing, painting, teaching, learning—we can be the creative people God intends. Middelmann has said it well: "A Christian understands that only in creative activity do we externalize the identity we have as men made in the image of God. This, then, is the true basis for work."[4]

9
Why Do I Need Other People?

DAVE HAD BEEN AROUND churches for a long time. He had visited almost every church and every youth group in our city in his attempt to discover himself. His need to be accepted became desperate at times. "Someday," he said, "I'll find out where I fit."

Dave and I talked a lot about his expectations for the Christian community. One day I asked the hard question, "Dave, could any group of believers—or any other group, for that matter—ever meet your needs?"

As the tears welled up, he sputtered, "Probably not! I need acceptance so badly I put a lot of pressure on people."

I tried to help Dave sort out some of his misconceptions about what the Christian community could and could not do for him. I asked him to answer one question for himself: "Why do I need people anyway?" This launched us into a discussion which was difficult but also very helpful.

What Others Can Do

We started with the positive because Scripture is clear that believers have a responsibility to one another. Dave had studied *Body Life*[1] and *Life Together*,[2] so he knew intellectually the importance of Christian community. But he rarely experienced the fellowship he read about, and when he did experience it, he made crumbs of it.

Others can encourage us. As we discussed what life in community can provide, we began with *encouragement*. At first Dave couldn't see any evidence that it was happening in his church. He needed it. He wanted it. But he just didn't feel that anyone was willing to encourage him.

Dave knew what the Scripture has to say about encouragement, but he had made the mistake of reading the Scripture backward. We looked at 1 Thessalonians 5:9-11 together. "For God did not appoint us to suffer wrath but to receive salvation through our Lord Jesus Christ. He died for us so that, whether we are awake or asleep, we may live together with him. Therefore encourage one another and build each other up, just as in fact you are doing."

As Dave read these verses he said, "They should be doing this for me. I need encouragement. I need to be built up." There was bitterness and disappointment in his voice. Dave was reading the Scripture backward—to justify his bitterness rather than to see how God wanted him to live. He had to move from what others should do to what he could do. The distance isn't far, but it is a rough trip to make.

"David," I said, "I know how badly you want encouragement, and I know God wants that for you. The problem is that things are never going to change until you change. You can't change others. You can only change yourself." We agreed on three steps he could take. First, he would confess his bitterness and ask God to unhook him from it each time it showed up. Second, he would read the Scripture frontward and do what he was commanded to do regardless of how others were behaving. Third, he would look for even the slightest bit of encouragement from others and savor it rather than crumbling it up as he had previously done.

Dave left my office skeptical and afraid, but at least he had a plan. When I next saw him he had some success to report. "I did some of the things we talked about," he said, "but I'm afraid I didn't do very well."

"No crumbs," I said. "I just want to hear what you did for yourself."

Dave reported that he had several times caught himself becoming bitter, and he had asked for God's help. He also said a couple of times he had just let the bitterness grow until he was hurt and angry. "All right," I said, "you are off to a good start. You were successful over half the time. That is a tremendous beginning."

Dave said, "Yeah, but—" and I stopped him before he could continue.

"David," I said, "I just offered you a cookie. I was encouraging you. Take it and enjoy your success. Don't make crumbs out of it."

Sheepishly he said, "I guess I was doing that, wasn't I."

"Yes," I said, "all I really needed to hear was 'thank you.' You deserved the cookie—enjoy it."

I asked how he did at encouraging others. "Okay," he said, "but I discovered something very interesting about myself. I don't know how to encourage. I just don't seem to know what to say, even when I want to encourage." Dave gave me a couple of examples, and I coached him by giving him ideas he might have used. Finally we decided that the golden rule from Matthew 7:12 might be helpful. We wrote our own version to apply it to encouragement: "Encourage others by saying and doing the kinds of things you would like them to say or do to you if you were in their circumstances."

This gave Dave a tool to use during the coming week, and it

also let me challenge him in a new way. "Dave," I asked, "in the past when people haven't encouraged you in the way you would have liked, what did you say to yourself about it?"

After a moment or two he said, "Well, I guess I told myself they didn't like me or they would have encouraged me."

"Now," I said, "after your experiences of trying to encourage others this week, do you know another possible reason why others haven't encouraged you?"

"That's funny," he said; "I never thought that others might not encourage me because they don't know how. I just assumed they didn't want to. I don't treat myself very nicely, do I?"

"No," I said, "you need to give yourself and others a break."

Dave said, "You know, if I think about that, it will probably help me with my bitterness. It makes me angry to think people don't care. I'm not nearly so angry if I think people don't know how."

"Dave," I said, "you do good work for yourself."

He started to reply and then muffled his words. Finally he laughed and said, "Thank you."

"You're welcome," I said. "I like cookies better than crumbs."

When we talked about receiving encouragement, Dave made more interesting discoveries. First, he began to realize that his brothers and sisters were not letting him down as much as he had thought. He also realized that he had made crumbs out of some of the encouragement he had received. "I can work on being more open to receive," he said, "but I still have one problem. Sometimes I feel so insecure that I want people to tell me I have made a good decision or I'm an OK person, and they just don't do it."

He was shocked when I said, "That's good!"

"How can that be good?" he asked.

"You cannot look outside yourself and expect others to stamp your ticket," I explained. "Your worth and approval must ultimately come from God and the strengthening of God's Spirit within you. It is nice when others say you are on target, but if all your validation comes from others' approval, you will be constantly frustrated."

"I don't know any other way," he said.

We decided on two questions he could ask himself: Do I believe this is a good choice? Am I being true to who I feel God wants me to be? "Dave," I said, "if you can say yes to both questions, give yourself a great big cookie and give God a big thank you."

Dave was on the way to learning how the body of Christ can be a source of encouragement, and he was also beginning to learn how to be an encourager himself.

Others can value us. Every day I am shocked by the ways human beings are devalued in our society. When I see how we treat each other, it is little wonder that most people have problems with self-esteem. I believe that Christianity lets us see mankind differently. Believers can see others the way God sees them—as special creations, unique and valuable. When we allow God to love and value others through us, we are truly his disciples. When we refuse to treat others this way, we are no longer being Christian. What gets in the way? Probably self-preservation. When I am trying to keep my own head above water, I may pull others down instead of lifting them up. God's plan is not for us to try to save ourselves, but for each to bear one another's burdens. When we move away from this plan we are in danger of going under.

For many years my good friend Ron has served as a model for me in the way he values people. I do not mean that he never becomes angry or disgusted with people. He can be insulted, frustrated or hurt just like anybody else. But Ron is unique in that he chooses to focus not on his hurts, but rather on the value he sees in those around him. Some say he has never met a stranger; this is because he wants to like every person he meets. He believes each person has value, and he wants to interact with the value he sees. Ron's life is richer because he has allowed God to develop his ability to value others, and certainly the lives of others are richer because he values them.

We are faced with a predicament: we are to value and love others, yet we know that people can hurt us. Do we dare risk reaching out to the stranger on the street? On the other hand, do we dare be less than God intended us to be? Scripture makes one thing perfectly clear. We are to value other members of the Christian community regardless of how different they are from us. Even when we do not like someone, we can still value him or her. As we try to value people, we may begin to appreciate their unique role in the Christian community. And as relationships develop, we will probably become more aware of our own self-worth as well as the value of the other.

We cannot remind ourselves too often of God's truth spoken in John 13:34-35: "A new commandment I give you: Love one another. As I have loved you, so you must love one another. All men will know that you are my disciples if you love one another."

Others can challenge us to live up to our potential. When you see the word *challenge,* what image pops into your mind? Maybe it is of someone shouting or pointing a finger at you. Maybe it is of someone quickly but sternly reading you the riot act. In either case it's someone telling you what you are doing wrong. I want to suggest a new image, one that is strongly supported by Scripture. This is the image of a group of Christians helping you define your potential and then telling you to go for it.

In 2 Timothy 4:2 we read these words: "Correct, rebuke and encourage—with great patience and careful instruction." One of the most helpful things another Christian can do for us is to challenge us to be all we can be. When I was beginning to be active in sports, I was discouraged when my coach told me what to do. I felt like I should already know how to play, and my self-esteem went down each time he approached me. I got myself in such a state of mind that I couldn't even receive his compliments. I was sure he thought I was a bad player and was just trying to make me feel better. When my dad noticed what I was going through, he said, "Have you noticed who the people are that the coach doesn't challenge?" As I thought about it, I realized that the coach was challenging the people who were starting the games. He was challenging the in-group, not the outsiders.

Hebrews 12:5-6 reminds us that even discipline, a harsh form of challenging, gives evidence of God's love for us: "My son, do not make light of the Lord's discipline, and do not lose heart when he rebukes you, because the Lord disciplines those he loves, and punishes everyone he accepts as a son." If God disciplines us to help us grow to be all we can be, then certainly we can help each other by saying, "Reach for your potential." I have often challenged people to use their teaching ability. On more than one occasion, those people have shed tears because they didn't know they had any ability to use. Wise Christians pray for strength to listen and respond to the challenges that come from the Christian community. Just as I found it hard to accept the fact that I didn't know everything about baseball, many people find it difficult to think they haven't yet reached their potential. But if they accept the challenge and continue to grow, their self-esteem will grow also. As one person said, "It is neat to be moving closer to who God made me to be."

Probably no area of body life requires more meekness and sensitivity than the area of challenging. People who have effectively challenged me are those whose primary message is "I care about you." Gentleness and empathy are the bywords (see Gal 6:1). We need to have a high regard for the value of others and a strong awareness of the fragility of human personality. "Be kind and compassionate to one another, forgiving each other, just as in Christ God forgave you" (Eph 4:32). David Augsburger gives a helpful guideline, "Caring enough to listen, to listen to the whole person, positive and negative, hurting and healing, is the heart of our human connection one to another. In listening we become truly *with* another. In caring we become truly *for* another. 'Being with' and 'being for' are the two central elements of loving relationship."[3] Don't be afraid to challenge others to reach the potential you see in them, and don't be afraid to receive challenges from others. Challenges will help you to discover yourself.

Others can complement us. Romans 12:1 challenges us to be all we can be by presenting our bodies as living sacrifices, pleasing to God. But that isn't enough. We are not just individual Christians. We are part of a body. God wants all of you, but he also wants all the other believers he has placed around you to complement or complete you.

Just as each of us has one body with many members, and these members do not all have the same function, so in Christ we who are many form one body, and each member belongs to all the others.We have different gifts, according to the grace given us. If a man's gift is prophesying, let him use it in proportion to his faith. If it is serving, let him serve; if it is teaching, let him teach; if it is encouraging, let him encourage; if it is contributing to the needs of others, let him give generously; if it is leadership, let him govern diligently; if it is showing mercy, let him do it cheerfully. (Rom 12:4-8)

Jim was a pastor who felt he had to be competent in everything. He got into trouble with his congregation when he tried to ramrod the new construction project through the board of elders. But he was clearly in over his head. One of the elders of the church took the risk of challenging him. Fortunately he listened to the challenge and backed off before permanent damage was done. He stuck to preaching, and one of the men who knew construction complemented him so that the work got done.

Look for ways to complement other believers, and don't be ashamed to ask them to complement you. This is the way God intended it. It is up to us to make it work.

Others can give us support. Diane, in her first year of college, has had a difficult time adjusting to the pressures. She has had trouble socially and academically. Her friends at church would like to help her, but they don't know what to do. One said, "Sometimes I am torn between letting her make it all on her own and taking over for her."

It is helpful to distinguish among the ideas of ignoring, carrying and supporting. Scripture implies that we are responsible to help our brothers and sisters. When Cain asked, "Am I my brother's keeper?" he expected a negative reply, but he didn't get one. For those who wish to live as committed Christians, ignoring others is clearly not an option. But Scripture does not ask us to carry others. When we carry, we assume the entire responsibility. The others don't have to do anything for themselves. They don't even have to hang on unless they are afraid of being dropped.

In contrast to ignoring and carrying, supporting requires that we stay close to others without assuming responsibility for them. People who are carried become weaker, not stronger. Paul Welter has pointed out the danger of doing too much for people. He writes, "The rescuer takes the responsibility away from the person being helped. It is as if we would say to a person, 'You can't handle this at all; let me do it for you.' This has the same effect as doing something for a child he could have done for himself with some guidance—it leaves him a little more helpless and considerably more resentful."[4]

While supporting others creates vitality within the body of Christ, carrying and ignoring result in weakness or despair. As long as Janet was willing to do Bill's math assignment, he never learned how to do it himself. Consequently his self-esteem was low. One day in frustration she said, "I'm not going to do it for you anymore, Bill. I'm not helping you; all I am doing is building up resentment." This was difficult for Janet to say; often it is as hard to refuse to carry as it is to refuse to be carried.

Janet stuck with her vow, however, and Bill got better at math. Needless to say, their relationship also improved. Bill said, "I never really wanted her to do it for me, but when I felt pressured I would go against my own best judgment. I felt rotten about myself and what I was doing to her."

There are ways to give support which will help ourselves as well as others.

1. Keep in contact with people; ask them how they are doing.

2. Help them set goals for themselves, and then follow up to see if they have met them.

3. Offer to be with them during difficult times. Our presence may be enough to help them realize they can make it.

4. Be willing to assist them in tasks which may be more than they can do alone.

5. Point out areas of progress and accomplishment, and do not let them make crumbs out of what they have done.

6. Pray specifically for their success, and let them know we are praying.

It took Dave a long time to realize the importance of his commitment to others and their role in his life. As he realized what others could do for him, he began to have more confidence in his ability to do things for them.

Things Others Cannot Do for Us

When I first saw Dave he was insisting that his Christian friends should be doing certain things for him. He wanted to force things to be a certain way, but he was having no success. He was miserable, and he was making others miserable as well. "Dave," I said, "you can't get blood out of a turnip. Let's talk about what others cannot do for you."

Others cannot give us value. People can value us, but they cannot give us value. We have inherent value because the Creator places value on us. You and I have to discover this value and claim it for ourselves. Others cannot do that for us. Sometimes it is easier to discover our God-given value if others say they value us, but no amount of effort on their part can take the place of the discovery we must make for ourselves.

Others cannot convince us that we have value. Margaret has been depressed for years. She has trouble seeing any value in herself. People value her. They like her. In fact, they like her much more than she likes herself. In despair she said, "I don't look at the evidence. It doesn't seem to matter that people care for me. I turn it off and act like it wasn't there. I can't stop devaluing myself even when others are trying to convince me that I have value to them."

Dave's problem was more subtle. He liked to hear positive things about himself, but he seemed insatiable. He couldn't get enough to fill himself up. Dave had to realize that no amount of being valued by others could take the place of acknowledging the value he saw in himself. If Dave would not accept himself as valuable, then others could not value him enough to help him get through the tough times.

I encouraged Dave to stop trying to elicit valuing statements from others and to begin to identify the things he valued in himself. At first it seemed foreign to him, almost unspiritual. But as Dave's self-image began to improve, he realized that by valuing himself, he was beginning to see himself as God saw him.

Others can't make us feel good. Most of us have at one time or another felt so bad we wished we could just die. Maybe we said, "If someone would just make me feel better." Forget it! It doesn't work! No one can make us feel better, and no one can make us feel bad. People can do nice things for us or they can mistreat us, but we feel bad because we choose to feel bad. And we feel good because we choose to feel good.

I do lots of things my wife likes, but she doesn't feel good all the time. In fact, much to my dismay, sometimes she feels good when I haven't done anything special, and she may feel bad even when I have. It depends on what she is choosing to focus on at the time. I need to do helpful things for her, but she alone can choose to be happy. Minirth and Meier have written, "It is difficult for many laymen to comprehend that anyone would choose unhappiness and depression over peace and happiness, but many people do so for a variety of reasons of which they are unaware. Some choose unhappiness to manipulate their mates and friends by enlisting their sympathies."[5]

To feel good, we can start by looking at the most stable things in life. "Jesus Christ is the same yesterday and today and forever"

(Heb 13:8). We can feel good knowing that God is there even when life has its ups and downs. Looking at the world we see all the beauty God has given us to enjoy. Taking a deep breath, we feel God restore us physically. Identifying someone we love or someone who loves us revives our self-worth. We can't focus on what we don't have and expect to feel good. Focusing on what we do have can generate thanks to God. Scripture makes a direct link between thankfulness and joy. Psalm 100, a psalm of thanksgiving, starts with a call to joyfulness and gladness:

Shout for joy to the LORD, all the earth.
Serve the Lord with gladness;
come before him with joyful songs.
Know that the LORD is God.
It is he who made us, and we are his;
we are his people, the sheep of his pasture.
Enter his gates with thanksgiving
and his courts with praise;
give thanks to him and praise his name.
For the LORD is good and his love endures forever;
his faithfulness continues through all generations.

Others can't make us feel good, but we can feel good if we choose to focus on a stable, caring God who has done good things for us. He may not have given us what we think would be perfect, but he has given us all we need.

Others can't make good choices for us. Self-esteem results from a series of good choices we make for ourselves. These choices lead us to live life so we experience God's blessing. Others can't make those choices for us.

I turned on my answering machine and grabbed a pad to take down telephone numbers. The first thing I heard was someone clearing his throat, then attempting to catch his breath and regain composure. Finally the voice came: "Dr. Wilson, this is Dan. I need you to call me."

I knew Dan was in trouble. I could hear his fear and disappointment even in the scratchy recording. I called immediately, and he answered at the first ring as though he had been sitting by the telephone.

"I've had a bad day," he said. "Everything came crashing down on me. Trying to feel better about myself, I let a guy I met talk me into taking some drugs. Now I feel horrible! I prayed and prayed that God would help me get home. I'm here, but I'm confused and afraid."

Dan's life is characterized by constant struggle. He is constantly confronted with choices which, if made in the wrong direction, could destroy his self-esteem and may even take his life. "I snorted some stuff," he said, "and I don't know for sure what it was." When Dan chooses to give control of his life to drugs or other people's desires, he loses sight of who God intended him to be. I can't make those choices for him, and neither can his fellowship group at church. His very life depends on whether or not he can begin to make better choices for himself.

Every person has to choose. The key question is this: By what or by whom are we going to be controlled?

"Everything is permissible for me"—but not everything is beneficial. "Everything is permissible for me"—but I will not be mastered by anything. "Food for the stomach and the stomach for food"—but God will destroy them both. The body is not meant for sexual immorality, but for the Lord, and the Lord for the body. By his power God raised the Lord from the dead, and he will raise us also. Do you not know that your bodies are members of Christ himself? Shall I then take the members of Christ and unite them with a prostitute? Never! Do you not know that he who unites himself with a prostitute is one with her in body? For it is said, "The two will become one flesh." But he who unites himself with the Lord is one with him in spirit. (1 Cor 6:12-17)

Dan wants to be controlled by Jesus Christ, but he has not been willing to make the choices necessary to allow that to happen. He wants others to offer him the protection that good choices bring, but the Christian community can only support him in those good choices; they cannot make them for him. Dan has taken some steps forward: he has told his small group of Christian friends that he wants to make good choices and that he needs them to pray that he will have the strength to do so.

Others can't take responsibility for our well-being. Dan's story helps us focus on another important issue. Christianity, more than any other religion, protects the integrity of the individual while offering the support of the community of believers. It is frustrating to see Dan on the brink of destruction. I ask myself constantly what I should do. I can be there for him, but I cannot take responsibility for his actions or his well-being. He will find himself and esteem himself only as he seeks God and makes appropriate choices. If I take too much responsibility for him, I end up carrying him. That may work for a while, but when I set him down he will be too weak to walk. If he is going to discover himself, he has to walk the road himself. At times he wants me to do more, but I can't. It is his life and he is living it. My role as a fellow Christian is to encourage, challenge, exhort, teach and support, but not to take the responsibility. It is a tough role to play, but it is the only option open. I pray for Dan's perseverance, and I pray for my ability to continue to be there.

Keeping Expectations under Control

When we know our needs and hope some of them will be met by our community of believers, it is easy to fall into the trap of uncontrolled expectations. But in dealing with other people, even Christians, we are dealing with people like ourselves—people with strengths and weaknesses.

Let's face it—we often want more from people than they know how to give. If we are looking to our Christian community for a cure for all our identity and self-esteem struggles, we are in for a three-story fall.

A bit of healthy skepticism may be helpful. Sometimes we can say, "The group can do at least this much for me, and I will focus on that and enjoy it." As we set our expectations for receiving from others, we will also need to set our expectations for giving to them. One of the greatest things a group can do for us is provide us with a place to be committed to others. Commitment to others is foundational to identity and to self-esteem. (See the first part of chapter six.)

One rule I have found invaluable in controlling my expectations is this: it is important to state my needs and to ask others to help, but I cannot demand that they do so. Myrna needed a lot of affection and support from her family. She expected her husband and children to see her needs and meet them. It wasn't happening. The more she wanted it, the less she shared her needs, and the more needy she became. She tried to turn to people in her church, but they could only do so much. She expected more than anyone could give, and, what was even worse, she expected them to know what she needed without her telling them. By the time I saw her, she was at the brink of despair. She began to reverse the insidious process when she took the risk of telling her husband what she needed rather than expecting he would know. It was difficult at first; he was defensive and didn't always know what to do to meet her needs, and Myrna would often slip back into focusing on what he was not doing rather than on the needs he was beginning to meet. Eventually, though, she acknowledged that the new approach was working and that she was feeling better. Her husband's comment said a lot: "Learning new patterns is hard for me, but it is worth it now that I know more of what she wants."

Another way to control expectations is to set small goals and rejoice when they are accomplished. I had to force Myrna to focus on the good things her husband was doing. Her temptation was to see only his weak areas. Why look for trouble? Seeing accomplishments, even small ones, can give us reason for rejoicing. "Rejoice in the Lord always. I will say it again: Rejoice!" (Phil 4:4).

Sometimes when people have been disappointed in relationships they make the opposite mistake of setting their expectations too low. Usually if we don't expect to receive much, that is exactly what we get. If we don't expect our friends to treat us with respect, they probably won't. On the other hand, if our standard is high but reachable and we are clear about what we need without being demanding, we may be pleasantly surprised. I have always enjoyed treating my wife like a lady, because from the time we met at age fourteen she has expected that of me. Sometimes I have failed and have disappointed myself and her. She hasn't thrown those failures in my face, but she has not lowered her expectations either. She has called me to be all I can be and to help her be all she can be. We can value ourselves enough to expect others to treat us like the people of value God created. Human dignity begins with knowing who created us; it continues as we discover the value of God's creative work. Let's expect others to recognize that dignity in you, expect to receive from them and expect to give to them. That is what Christian community is all about.

A Healthy Christian Community
A Christian community cannot do everything for us, but it can certainly help us as we grow in Christ. I have discovered seven characteristics of Christian community which are vital for growth and health.

Positive proclamation of the love of Christ. Let's face it—if God didn't love us, we would be without hope! "This is how God showed his love among us: He sent his one and only Son into the world that we might live through him. This is love: not that we loved God, but that he loved us and sent his Son as an atoning sacrifice for our sins. Dear friends, since God so loved us, we also ought to love one another" (1 Jn 4:9-11). If awareness of this love is not central, the Christian community will falter and be less than God intended. Look for a place where the message resonates loud and clear. "God loves you, and I love you."

Emphasis on following the Savior and the leading of Scripture. Christian community without divine authority will fail. Saying "Amen" and "Praise the Lord" is not enough. A healthy community tries to emulate the Savior's character and discipline. Unless we follow Christ and the leading of Scripture, we are vulnerable to misguided human persuasiveness. We have only to look at the explosion of modern cults to realize the dangers of following humans rather than God. As the saying goes, "Let the buyer beware." Be skeptical about others' brand of faith until we can determine whether they are following the Jesus of Scripture or some God of their own creation. It isn't enough just to know it makes us feel good to be with them. The devil himself has an uncanny ability to make people comfortable. Search for the love that lasts. The guidebook for such love is the Holy Bible.

Emphasis on the importance of the individual. When I hear people uttering the same phrases or wearing the same clothing I become uncomfortable. When Jesus chose the disciples, he chose a diverse group. They didn't look alike and they didn't act alike. In fact, they didn't always get along. Because they were strong individuals, they were able to move the world.

When Christian groups demand that individuality be surrendered, they are tampering with identity. They are destroying a God-given strength. God could have cloned Jesus Christ. We could have all been perfect. But he had a better plan. God values our diversity, and we are to value the diversity in our Christian community. This is not always easy, but it is healthy. Individuality is God's own check-and-balance system. I am not preaching a brand of secular humanism; I am simply saying that individuality is important and must be protected and nurtured. "God has arranged the parts in the body, every one of them, just as he wanted them to be. If they were all one part, where would the body be? As it is, there are many parts, but one body" (1 Cor 12:18-20). If you are comfortable in your group simply because everyone is alike, you may be paying too high a price for comfort. There is a difference between a common bond in Christ and a community based on fear of being different.

Personal encouragement. We have placed heavy emphasis upon encouragement throughout this book because it is so essential to Christian growth. Don't get caught in a group without it. Support groups need to stress the importance of the person in the same way that Scripture does. Notice the sensitivity mandated in 2 Timothy 4:2: "Encourage—with great patience and careful instruction." We need the kind of encouragement that prepares individuals to encourage themselves. Encouragement that respects the person is encouragement that says, "Follow the Savior and be all he has made you to be."

Exhortation without motivation by guilt. People need to know when they are straying from the path God says they are to walk. What they do not need is to be told that because of what they are doing others will stray, God's reputation will be ruined, babies will die, souls will go to hell, parents' reputations will be ruined, churches will have to close their doors, evil will triumph and so on and so on and so on. Don't get me wrong. Bad things happen when we sin. The problem is that many Christian groups work so hard at making people feel guilty about what they have done that they never help them find a better alternative. The Bible says go for the good. It does not say spend forever wallowing in guilt over the bad you have done. Jesus in his mercy simply told people to go and sin no more. He didn't waste time trying to increase their level of guilt or make them pay for their sins. People who met Jesus were able to say they were wrong without feeling that they could never make up for it.

Celebration of victory, not preoccupation with defeat. I believe there are lots of parties in heaven—celebrations involving angels and mankind. Scripture says that the angels rejoice over one sinner who comes to Christ (see Lk 15:7).

Let's have a party when someone comes to Christ. Let's rejoice when lives are turned Godward. Let's kill the fatted calf when the wayward son returns. Let's praise God when Scott decides not to get drunk this weekend.

How much time does your group spend on victories? How much time does it spend on defeats? We talk about what we value—I want to be involved with a group that talks about the positive and celebrates God's victories in our lives. I want to talk about life. I don't have any trouble remembering the realities of death.

A worshiping community. Underlying the six characteristics of healthy groups we have mentioned is an attitude of adoration for the Savior. A healthy group worships him, both formally and informally.

If your group isn't a worshiping group, then it has lost sight of its very purpose. The psalmist wrote:

It is good to praise the LORD
    and make music to your name, O Most High,
to proclaim your love in the morning
    and your faithfulness at night,
to the music of the ten-stringed lyre
    and the melody of the harp.
For you make me glad by your deeds, O LORD;
    I sing for joy at the works of your hands.
How great are your works, O LORD,
    how profound your thoughts! (Ps 92:1-5)

Nothing is as conducive to mental health, identity and self-esteem than worship. It is the glue that binds us together within our own souls and as people who need the Father and each other.

10
Discovering Myself

A PROBLEM WITH A BOOK designed to increase self-understanding is that it may end up giving more information than we know what to do with. This could be discouraging, which would certainly not please either the reader or the author. Knowledge that is not acted on may turn out to be more a curse than a blessing. With this predicament in mind, I have developed several steps you can take in response to what you have read in the previous chapters. These steps are not cure-alls, but beginning places They are not magic, they are aids. You will have already taken some of the steps while others may have escaped you completely. Don't waste time worrying about what hasn't happened; invest your energies in what can be.

Attack False Beliefs

When Susan first came to see me, she was depressed and suicidal. Her self-acceptance was at the lowest ebb of her thirty years of life. "I don't like me," she said, "and I don't see how anyone else could stand me either." I began to help her discover herself by examining her relationship with God. She had all the right theological answers, but at the emotional level she believed God had forsaken her because of her sin. Her theology said, "God forgives sinners," but her feelings said, "He abandons." Susan attacked this false belief by going back to Scripture. "God has said, 'Never will I leave you; never will I forsake you' " (Heb 13:5).

I encouraged Susan to deal with her feelings of abandonment by praising God that her feelings were incorrect. When she felt unforgiven, she learned to praise God for the forgiveness the Bible said was hers. It was difficult, but her feelings began to change. One day she said, "You know, since you made me praise God whether I felt like it or not, I have realized that my whole prayer life during the past year was self-pity. God hadn't abandoned me; he just wasn't taking part in my self-pity."

If God seems far away, we should check to see who has the new address. Susan's relationship with God began to recover as she began to read the Bible again. I directed her to passages like Psalm 139 which reveal that we are God's creation: "I praise you because I am fearfully and wonderfully made; your works are wonderful, I know that full well" (v. 14). More difficult than accepting God's view of her as a special creation was acknowledging what she liked about herself. Others could see good things about her; she could see only flaws. Her mind had to be retrained. I encouraged her to tell me things she enjoyed about herself. At first the list was small. Later she was able to see herself in a more positive light. I recognized a breakthrough when she was able to say, "You know, I used to hate myself for getting so concerned over other people's problems. Now I realize that being sensitive can be a good characteristic." It isn't easy to enjoy ourselves when we have been taught self-hatred. It isn't easy, but it is essential if we are to discover ourselves.

When people lose sight of who they are, they also lose sight of their gifts. As Bill said, "I was afraid to believe I had gifts for fear I would use them and then they would be taken away." I encouraged Bill to use his gift of friendship by developing a relationship with a junior-high student. Bill was amazed at the results. "The guy is coming alive," he said, "and I am beginning to feel some new life in me at the same time."

Susan found it especially difficult to use her gifts because she had been told all her life she couldn't do anything right. She had natural abilities as a teacher, but had not employed them because of her fear of being criticized. "That would be awful if you were criticized," I chided. "You would probably have a mental breakdown."

"No," she said, "but I wouldn't like it." Later she said, "You know, if I avoid all the things I don't like, my life won't be worth much."

Susan began to help teach a class at the local recreation center. This helped her to regain her confidence; later she was able to take full responsibility for a class herself. "Who are you?" I asked. She looked puzzled for a moment and then smiled. "I am a teacher," she said, "and I think I'm becoming a pretty good one."

Correct One Bad Habit

Beginning to use our gifts is an essential part of discovering who we are. It is unnatural at first. It's like a baby bird trying to use its wings or a colt learning to walk. However, as the muscles are tested they become stronger, and we begin to catch the excitement of soaring or running. On the other hand, when we haven't discovered ourselves, we are as awkward and unsure as a fish out of water. Our perception of God and ourselves goes out of focus, and we find it difficult to use our gifts. We also develop bad habits—not bad habits like improper eating or smoking, but bad habits in our way of relating to other people and perceiving ourselves.

Jim's life is an example of this. Because he had not discovered himself, he became frightened in social situations and withdrew. Henry said, "I would like to get to know him better, but he won't let me." Jim's habit of withdrawing was keeping him from discovering himself through relationships.

When I confronted him with this problem, he said, "The sad part is that I really am starved for friendships." He even admitted a strong desire to get to know Henry. We agreed that Jim should try to move toward people whether he felt like it or not. Jim started by approaching some of the people he felt most comfortable with and worked up to approaching strangers. It wasn't long before people began to encourage him by telling him how much they enjoyed him. Although he couldn't accept their compliments at first, he eventually grew to see them as genuine and valuable.

Sally also developed an unwanted habit that took root during a period of low self-esteem. She had become a traveling cactus—she would go from person to person or group to group seeking approval. Unfortunately when people reached out to her, all they touched was thorns. She assured me that no one accepted her, and soon her life proved her words. People stop giving approval when they get consistently attacked in return.

I didn't have to convince Sally that she was hurting people. She already knew that. What she did not know was that she could relate to people without her prickly armor. When she decided to give up being hostile and nasty, she felt helpless and vulnerable, uncertain that she could survive. However, she soon began to feel encouraged as people began to reach out to her again and did not choose to hurt her.

Sometimes the bad habits are personal rather than interpersonal. When we feel bad about ourselves, we may make poor choices about our use of time. Mike said, "Last week I went to six movies, and not one of them was something I really wanted to see." Susan retreated to television. Sam started drinking every evening. Bill stopped working out at the gym, even though it was usually a highlight for him. Jill started sleeping more.

These bad habits must be overcome if you are to discover yourself. Choose one and attack it. Mary's habit was overeating. When I challenged her to attack it, she put a sign on the refrigerator door which read, "Once on the lips, forever on the hips." Much later she was able to say, "I have finally learned that being fat doesn't have to be a part of who I am."

Please note that I said, "Correct *one* bad habit." We don't need to correct all our bad habits, or even two of them. We do not need to take on the whole world; we do, however, need to get headed in the right direction. One of the great principles of behavior change is to tackle problems in small segments so we can achieve some success. Self-control comes one step at a time. When we have succeeded in correcting one bad habit, we will have greater energy to take on the next one. The first step is always the hardest. The key is to do it whether we feel like it or not.

Bury the Past

Larry was a good client who tried to follow all my suggestions. He had no trouble identifying a bad habit and attacked it diligently. He seemed to be successfully moving toward self-discovery. Then one day he called me in tears and said, "I just can't take it anymore. I'm overwhelmed. I'm doing so well, but I'm feeling so bad." The more we talked, the clearer it became that Larry was in mourning for a girlfriend who had recently left him for someone else. Each time he started to feel good about himself, he would say, "But what's the use? If I don't have her, my life has no meaning."

One day I asked Larry to take a walk with me. When he asked where we were going, I said, "To the graveyard. It is time for a funeral. You need to accept once and for all the fact that Pam is gone. There is nothing you can do about it." Larry knew he was angry and disappointed. But he also needed to recognize that losing Pam did not mean he was any less of a person.

The eulogy was an important part of the mourning process for Larry. He needed to recognize that his relationship with Pam had been good and valuable to both of them, even though it hadn't ended with their living together happily ever after. Unfortunately he had been taught that a relationship is not good unless it is permanent. Larry came to recognize that God had used Pam to help him grow, and that God had also used him in Pam's life. When he saw the good that had come out of their relationship, he wrote Pam a letter wishing her well and thanking her for touching his life.

Giving up a disappointment is a difficult but necessary part of discovering who we are. By going through this process Larry discovered that he didn't have to be bitter anymore. He also learned that he was stronger than he might have been had he not met Pam. There is an important lesson here. Just because ham and eggs are good and make us grow doesn't mean we should eat ham and eggs the rest of our lives. Sometimes we need to give up ham and eggs in order to discover the joy of, say, waffles and strawberries.

Almost all my clients who have low self-esteem have had to give up some disappointment before going on to greater self-discovery. Funerals are never pleasant, but for the mourner they can signal the start of a new life. You give up the past and make a new commitment to the future. It is especially difficult to give up the past when we have disappointed ourselves. One of the most debilitating phrases I know is, "I should have known better." Long after we have let ourselves down, we continue to crush ourselves with the burden of omniscience and omnipotence. "I should have known better" and "I should have been stronger" do not change today. If anything, they restrict today even more.

Face the facts—you blew it. You made a mistake. You didn't win. You failed to reach your goal. The crucial question is this: Are you going to see yourself as only these past failures, or are you going to accept the challenge of living again? Have a funeral for your failure, and then focus on future possibilities. It is your failure that needs to be put in the casket, not you. Jesus said, "Go, and sin no more" (Jn 8:11 KJV). Whether the problem is sin or failure, we often need to begin again. You don't expect other people to be perfect—give yourself the same break.

Accept Help from Friends

I have made lots of promises to myself. The problem is that I am not always strong enough to keep my promises. I need someone else to hold me accountable. That is what friends are for. As we discover ourselves, we will need some person or persons to keep us from reverting to our old habits and to help us follow through with our new goals. One way they will need to hold us accountable is to keep us from making crumbs. It is easy to develop a habit of downgrading ourselves and failing to accept who others say we are.

Just last evening my wife said, "You look nice." My reflex comment was, "I'll look better when I lose a little weight." She caught me immediately. "You might look better thinner," she said, "but don't make crumbs out of the compliment I just gave you. You look nice." Who wants to argue with that? A thank-you was the only appropriate response.

When people downgrade themselves or make crumbs out of the cookies others offer them, they are often playing a false humility game. A friend who is a nurse was about to draw blood from a patient when he asked, "Are you good at this?"

"Very good," she replied.

The patient then relaxed and said, "That's a relief. I don't want anyone but an expert taking my blood."

When people acknowledge our skills or when we recognize an area of competence, we shouldn't be afraid to enjoy the awareness of that plus. We don't have to brag, but we don't have to deny the positive characteristic either. Eating cookies is better than making crumbs.

A good friend will help us celebrate as we grow toward our

potential. I believe every person needs a growth buddy. Kay and Sandy have that kind of relationship. They pray together and support each other during defeats, and they celebrate the victories. "I think I grew some today," Sandy said. "I wanted to keep my temper when I was criticized by the children, and I did it."

Kay's response was a jubilant hug. "I knew you could!" she said. Sandy and Kay have learned the biblical principle of weeping with those who weep and rejoicing with those who rejoice (Rom 12:15).

People have difficulty celebrating growth because of the pressure of perfectionism. We have been damaged by child-rearing patterns that communicate that we will have value only when we reach the top. Sandy and I have tried to let our son Michael know that we value his participation in sports whether he wins or loses. We are pleased he has chosen to condition his body and take the risk of losing. He doesn't always hear our acceptance, and sometimes he translates words of encouragement such as "you can win" into "you must win." But we want to challenge him to search for his potential without downgrading himself if he falls short of perfection.

Recently Mike's wrestling coach was most helpful. After Mike had lost a close match, Coach Burton said, "I have no complaints. You did everything we ask you to do. Don't worry about the mistakes. Experience will take care of them." The understanding coach helped Mike celebrate his potential even in the shadow of the loss. The win-at-all-cost philosophy robs us of the joy of celebrating the steps of progress along the way.

Enjoy Yourself

One reason it is hard to celebrate each step of progress is that some of those steps require us to do things we don't enjoy doing. My father taught me to enjoy the things I had to do. I never remember him complaining, even though as a farmer he often had to do unpleasant tasks. His example was very valuable to me. If I can enjoy what I am doing, I can also enjoy who I am.

I have tried to train myself to say "I get to mow the lawn," rather than "I have to mow the lawn." Changing the phrase doesn't make the lawn any smaller, but it changes me. If I get to mow the law, I just might have a good time doing it. I can relax and enjoy the smell of the newly mown grass or the sight of the blue sky. I can appreciate the fact that my efforts are making the yard more attractive. I might even decide to pull off my shirt and go for that elusive tan. On the other hand, if I have to mow the lawn, I will look only for misery. I'll concentrate on my aching back and the great sacrifice I am making to please other people. I probably won't notice that a robin has built a nest in the cherry tree. My whole day might turn into a case of poor me. I can choose which scenario to follow. If I choose "I get to," I feel I'm in greater control of my destiny.

Some people struggle with "I have to be me." In other words, being me is a horrible fate, but what can I do about it? There is another way to look at it. Being me is a privilege. In fact, I'm the only person in the whole world who can do it. Even on days when I am frustrated or have problems, I remind myself that I am the only person in the world who can work through the frustrations or solve the problems. Life becomes a challenge rather than a drag. When I visited New York City by myself, I was lonely and began to feel sorry for myself. "I don't even have anyone to eat dinner with," I lamented. Then the idea came— why not enjoy eating dinner by myself? I can tell myself all the things I like about the restaurant. I can point out the people I find interesting, and I can even discuss the food with myself. The only hard part was keeping my voice down.

We may think that sane people don't talk to themselves, but I believe just the opposite is true. Sane people do talk to themselves. In fact, we have to talk to ourselves to stay sane. As we tell ourselves what we like and dislike and as we soak up the experience we are having, we discover ourselves. We also give ourselves permission to be who we are.

By the way—not once was I interrupted. I could talk all I

wanted, and no one cared. I am not recommending isolationism. I am just saying that it was good to enjoy being with myself. I don't need other people to entertain me all the time.

The final step in discovering ourselves takes us back to the beginnings. Who am I? An adopted child of God, one of his loved ones. What is my purpose? Jesus replied: " 'Love the Lord your God with all your heart and with all your soul and with all your mind.' This is the first and greatest commandment. And the second is like it: 'Love your neighbor as yourself' (Mt 22:37-39). As I seek to live out this commandment, I realize I have value. Value to God, value to my neighbor and value to me. This is a great discovery. I have something to offer right now. That offering is me.

This is a vital insight. But it is also an insight that is hard to maintain. It requires dedication and regular communication with God. We can establish a daily pattern of worship in which we praise God for the work he is doing in our lives. It is time for us to stop denying his presence in our lives and to stop feeling bad about the things that are not the way we would like them. God has made us to love and praise him. As we do this, we begin to discover who we really are.

Notes

Chapter 1: Is Self-Worth Unchristian?

[1]S. Bruce Narramore, *You're Someone Special* (Grand Rapids, Mich.: Zondervan, 1978), p. 48.

[2]*Webster's Seventh New Collegiate Dictionary,* "Selfish" (Springfield, Mass.: G. & C. Merrian, 1972).

[3]Paul A. Hauck, *How to Stand Up for Yourself* (Philadelphia: Westminster, 1979), p. 67.

Chapter 2: What Is an Identity Crisis?

[1]Erik H. Erikson, *Identity, Youth and Crisis* (New York: W. W. Norton, 1968), p. 16.

[2]Eugene Kennedy, *If You Really Knew Me Would You Still Like Me?* (Niles, Ill.: Argus, 1975), p. 20.

[3]Carl R. Rogers, *On Becoming a Person* (Boston: Houghton-Mifflin, 1961).

[4]Robert E. Alberti and Michael L. Emmons, *Your Perfect Right,* 2nd ed. (San Luis Obispo, Calif.: Impact, 1974), p. 5.

[5]Narramore, *You're Someone Special,* p. 129.

Chapter 3: Basic Components of Identity

[1]Os Guinness, *In Two Minds* (Downers Grove, Ill.: InterVarsity Press, 1976), p. 111.

Chapter 4: Steps to Understanding Me

[1]James W. Sire, *The Universe Next Door* (Downers Grove, Ill.: InterVarsity Press, 1976), pp. 16-17.

[2]Paul A. Hauck, *How to Do What You Want to Do* (Philadelphia: Westminster, 1976), pp. 28-29.

[3]J. Grant Howard, *Balancing Life's Demands* (Portland: Multnomah, 1983), p. 14.

[4]Michael J. Mahoney, in *Handbook of Rational Emotive Therapy,* Albert Ellis and Russell Grieger, eds. (New York: Springer, 1977), p. 354.

Chapter 5: Can I Choose Who I Want to Be?

[1]Richard C. Nelson, *Choosing a Better Way to Live* (North Palm Beach, Fla.: Guidelines, 1977), p. xi.

[2]Earl D. Wilson, *The Undivided Self* (Downers Grove, Ill.: InterVarsity Press, 1983).

[3]Hauck, *How to Do What You Want to Do,* pp. 74-75.

Chapter 6: Becoming the Sum of My Commitments

[1]Donald Bridge and David Phypers, *Spiritual Gifts and the Church* (Downers Grove, Ill.: InterVarsity Press, 1973), pp. 158-59.

[2]Norman Wakefield, *Listening* (Waco, Tex.: Word, 1981), p. 17.

Chapter 7: Created to Grow

[1]Arnold Lazarus and Allen Fay, *I Can If I Want To* (New York: Warner, 1975), p. 15.

[2]Kennedy, *If You Really Knew Me,* pp. 35-36.

[3]Victor Raimy, *Misunderstandings of the Self* (San Francisco: Jossey-Bass, 1975), p. 9.

[4]Lazarus and Fay, *I Can If I Want To,* pp. 16-17.

[5]Hauck, *How to Do What You Want to Do,* p. 63.

[6]Charles R. Swindoll, *Starting Over* (Portland: Multnomah, 1977), pp. 26-27.

Chapter 8: Identity and Self-Worth in a High-Tech Society

[1]John L. Holland, *Making Vocational Choices* (Englewood Cliffs, N.J.: Prentice-Hall, 1973), p. 85.

[2]Udo Middelmann, *Pro-Existence* (Downers Grove, Ill.: InterVarsity Press, 1974), pp. 20-21.

[3]Ibid., p. 29.

[4]Ibid., p. 36.

Chapter 9: Why Do I Need Other People?

[1]Ray C. Stedman, *Body Life* (Glendale, Calif.: Regal, 1977).

[2]Dietrich Bonhoeffer, *Life Together* (New York: Harper and Row, 1976).

[3]David Augsburger, *Caring Enough to Hear* (Ventura, Calif.: Regal, 1982), p. 166.

[4]Paul Welter, *How to Help a Friend* (Wheaton, Ill.: Tyndale, 1978), p. 36.

[5]Frank B. Minirth and Paul D. Meier, *Happiness Is a Choice* (Grand Rapids, Mich.: Baker, 1978), p. 13.